BENEDICT SPINOZA

CREATIVE MULTIVERSE: NEW EXPLORATIONS IN TRANSFORMATIVE LEARNING AND RESEARCH

There is an epochal challenge of learning from multiple experiments in self and social transformations now. *Creative Multiverse* seeks to explore and present different pathways of transformations in societies and histories around the world. It builds upon engagements in learning in different disciplines of life and academy and seeks to create a transdisciplinary space of research, dialogues and transformations.

A Series from Shipra Publications, Delhi
Email: info@shiprapublications.com

Editor: Ananta Kumar Giri,
Madras Institute of Development Studies, Chennai, India.
Email: aumkrishna@yahoo.com; Website: www.mids.ac.in/ananta.htm

International Editorial Advisory Board

BENEDICT SPINOZA

An Appreciation

Chitta Ranjan Das

SHIPRA

ISBN: 978-81-7541-472-3

Price: Rs. 495; US$ 28

First Published in India in 2009

Benedict Spinoza: An Appreciation

Published by:
SHIPRA PUBLICATIONS
115-A, Vikas Marg, Shakarpur, Delhi-110092, INDIA
Phone: 91-11-65277210, 91-11-22500954
Fax: 91-11-22458662
E-mail: info@shiprapublications.com
www.shiprapublications.com

Foreword

Walking With Spinoza and Polishing Our Stubborn Lenses

Here in the twilight the translucent
Of the Jew polishing the crystal glass
The dying afternoon is cold with bands
Of Fear. Each day the afternoons all pass
The same. The hands and space of hyacinth
Palling in the confines of the ghetto walls
Barely exists for the quiet man who stalls
There, dreaming up a brilliant labyrinth.
Fame doesn't trouble him (that reflection of Dreams in the dream
of another mirror),
nor love,
The timid love women. Gone the bars,
He's free, from metaphor and myth, to sit
Polishing a stubborn lens: the infinite
Map of the One who knows is all His stars

—Jorge Louis Borges (1999), "Spinoza," in *Selected Poems*, p. 229.

Joy is man's passage from a less to a greater perfection [..] I say passage, for joy is not perfection in itself.

—Spinoza (2001), *Ethics*, p. 147.

Light can stream into the clearing, into its openness, and let brightness play with darkness in it. But light never first creates the clearing. Rather, light presupposes it. [..] It is necessary for thinking to become explicitly aware of [..] clearing [..] which sets us the task of learning from it while questioning it. [..]

The meditative man is to experience the untrembling heart of unconcealment. [..] It means uncealment itself in what is most its own, means the place of stillness that gathers in itself what first grants unconcealment. [..] the path of thinking, speculative and intuitive, needs the traversable clearing. But in that clearing rests

> possible radiance, that is, the possible presencing of presence itself. [..]
>
> Accordingly, we may suggest that the day will come when we will not shun the question whether the clearing, free openness , may not be that within which pure space and ecstatic time and everything present and absent in them have the place that gathers and protects everything.
>
> —Martin Heidegger (2004), "The End of Philosophy and the Task of Thinking," pp. 442-445.

I

Spinoza born as Baruch Spinoza in a Jewish neighborhood in Amsterdam in 1629 is an unacknowledged father of modern man who traversed many difficult paths in many fields-in matters of reason, religion, theology, polity, society, cosmos, Nature, God and ethics—and inspires us to undertake our own multiple journeys of self-realization, world realization and God-realization. I recall warmly my visit to *Spinoza Huis* (Spinoza House) near Leiden five years ago in a cold afternoon in December 2003 and felt the presence of this inspiring experimenter of humanity in his room where he was polishing lenses. But Spinoza was not polishing lenses for earning his bread only he was also polishing lenses of conventional modes of seeing and being. In the Spinoza House as I was signing my name in the register I saw the name of many other visitors down the ages including that of Albert Einstein who had said that his God is that of Spinoza.[1] Walking out of the house and looking at the sky with stars slowly exuding their radiance I felt Spinoza and the stars right in our midst, the infinite within ourselves. The next day visiting the house in which Spinoza lived in The Hague in front of which there is a statute of this meditative and penetrating thinker who looks you into your own eyes asking whether you realize that you are part of eternity, this vast Nature and God I felt the co-presence of Benedict Spinoza as well as Chitta Ranjan Das who more than twenty-five years ago had told me about Spinoza and had recently written to me that when I was in Europe I must not miss visiting Spinoza. We are grateful to Das now for gifting us this book of him on Spinoza which helps us to co-walk with this great thinker and thus realize our creative multiverse of learning, self-transformation and world transformation.

Chitta Ranjan Das, like Spinoza, is a meditative thinker and experimenter and in his present age of eighty five continues his *tapasya* of self-transformation and world transformation. Das had written this thesis on Spinoza sixty years ago in 1948 when he was only twenty-five as a student at Shantiniketan but this is a pearl of wisdom-- search and sharing, of philosophical engagement as an integral part of self-engagement and world-engagement. It presents us a lucid exposition of Spinoza's philosophy as well as his exemplary life and helps us to realize how reading Spinoza is to walk with him, polish our lenses, especially of reason, religion, and polity, and live with eternity in our very moments of every day lives.[2] Though Das does not polish lenses literally for a living he does work with our modes of seeing and strives to clean our mirrors as a student of life—his as well as ours-- and not to dump it under heaps of nails and weapons. As he writes in his foreword to *Nakha Darpanena*:[3] "The courageous people seek mirrors, strive to see things in the light of mirrors and also oneself."

In a recent introduction to Spinoza's classic *Ethics* Don Garrett writes:

> In the history of Western philosophy, few figures since Socrates himself have exerted so powerful an appeal on the imagination as does the figure of Spinoza. He captures the imagination as the quintessential philosopher, a solitary thinker of frail constitution whose hours of study and writing in his rented room are interrupted only for the lens-grinding that earns him his modest livelihood. He goes by the name of "Benedict de Spinoza," using the Latin equivalent of the given name ("Baruch," meaning "blessed") that he discarded in his youth following his excommunication by the Amsterdam Jewish community of his birth. Little concerned with wealth, fame, or the transitory pleasures that drive others, he is motivated by the pure love of truth to probe the deep identity of God with Nature and, in doing so, to achieve a union with God-or-Nature that is to be supremely rational and yet also seemingly tinged with mysticism.

The book in our hand, *Benedict Spinoza: An Appreciation*, probably the first one by an Indian scholar on this perennial thinker, helps us understand Spinoza's many-splendored works and life as he lived like a "student" inspiring us not only to live like a student but also be students of life. Das helps us understand Spinoza's concepts such as Substance, Mode, Attributes, Affects, Intuition, etc. Das also carries out a creative comparative global philosophical engagement in understanding Spinoza where he discusses Spinoza's work along with philosophers and sages in both Western and Eastern traditions such as Buddha, Shankara and Nietzsche. But in this Das is not reductive and he does not just compare East and West rather helps us see the quest for Truth manifest in different seekers and thinkers whether they come from East or West. It is remarkable how a young man of twenty-five had thought so insightfully about the human predicament and our ways of moving beyond.

Das's first published essay as a young man of nineteen was on Socrates and apart from this work on Spinoza Das has gifted us more than two hundred books on different aspects of life, education, literature and spiritual transformations including biographies and philosophical-literary discussions on such savants as Swami Vivekananda, Sri Aurobindo, Gandhi, Tagore, Tolstoy, Kristen Kold, Bhima Bhoi, Achyutananda Das, Arakhita Das and Iswara Chandra Vidyasagar.[4]

II

In this book Das tells us how Spinoza has inspired many poets, scientists and philosophers down the ages such as Goethe, Einstein, Thoreau and Nietzsche. There is also a creative engagement with Spinoza in contemporary liberatory vision and practice. For example, in charting pathways of an alternative democracy, Michael Hardt and Antonio Negri draw upon Spinoza. As Hardt writes:

> [For Spinoza] Democracy is to be the absolute, unlimited form of government, because in it the Supreme Power is fully constituted by the power of the multitude. Spinoza's democracy is to be animated by a constituent Power, a dynamic form of popular authority [..] In effect democracy is a return to a plane of the *Ethics*: Power (*potentia*) does not exist in Spinoza's democracy except to the extent that it is a constituent Power completely and freely constituted by the power of the multitude [..] If *Ethics* reduces the distinction and subordinates Power [Sovereign Power, for example] to power in the idealistic terms of its utopian vision, the *Political Treatise* poses the real tendency toward a

> future reduction of the distinction, when a democratic power would be completely constituted by the power of the multitude (Hardt 1991: xvi).

In a recent reflection on power, Das also shares with us the following about Spinoza which has the potential to transform our existing conceptions of self, knowledge and power:

> Benedict Spinoza has spoken about *Potestas* and *Potentia* – words both of which in the Latin language mean power. They are different in their import because they point out to different connotations. The former is functionally the urge to possess by bossing it over others and *potentia* reminds us about the potentials inherent in every human being, the many possibilities of flowering up and unfolding, if freedom is the climate in which it develops. According to Spinoza, love is the mediating link between knowledge and power. Love of humanity, love of the world, a deep faith in the unending possibilities of individuals as well as the collectives. This calls for a higher consciousness which all knowledge should congenially aim at.[5]

Spinoza urges us to transform power as realization of potential--self, other as well as social; this is a significant contribution to a deepened democracy at the contemporary juncture. As Arne Naess interprets Spinoza, "Power over others tends in the direction of limiting others right to unfold their nature" (Naess 1999: 49). For Spinoza, "The more we unfold the manifold (or many-side) of our nature, the more we are in ourselves (in suo esse), and the higher degree of freedom we achieve. This kind of development is experienced by joy, one's world is colored by joy, or more precisely is more joyful" (ibid: 48). Spinoza not only helps us to transform power and realize our potential but also to realize that as individuals we are not just isolated individuals, even our bodies are not solely our own; we have a dimension of transindividual within ourselves the realization of which would enhance the realization of what Jurgen Habermas calls "solidary praxis" in society (cf. Habermas 2003). Spinoza also inspires us to embody imagination in a new way, especially collective imagination overcoming the contemporary pathologies of reason and religion.

To understand the epochal relevance of Spinoza we can here refer to the debate between Jurgen Habermas, the pre-eminent critical theorist of our times, and Cardinal Joseph Ratzinger (and now Pope Benedict XVI) held nearly five years ago.[6] In this debate Habermas acknowledges the pathology of reason as it has been a slave to scientism and state power and Ratzinger the pathology of religion as it becomes a handmaiden to terror. Habermas and Ratzinger urge us to realize that what is needed at the contemporary juncture is a "correlation of reason and faith, of reason and religion, both being summoned to mutual cleansing and healing." In this task of cleansing and healing we can walk with and draw inspiration from Spinoza who worked as a doctor of human affects and pleader for more understanding beyond quick judgment, and not only Kant—who seems to be the primary source of inspiration with Habermasian critical theory.

Spinoza stressed the significance of reason in religion[7] and challenged us to go beyond superstition. Spinoza also sought to heal the split between "natural knowledge" and "divine knowledge" with ease. For Spinoza, "[..] 'natural knowledge' that is attainable by all human beings through the excess of their own natural faculties is really equivalent to prophecy, namely, that unique communication of 'sure knowledge of some matter revealed by God to human beings' [..]" (Bagley 2008: 15). As Das explains it in this book:

> Reason leads us to religion. Union with men by social piety raises us to feel the spirit of God. Men are not to be considered as so many worms or insects. We can only unite with them as one among them. To know this, to know oneself *sub specie aeternitatis* leads us to the intellectual love of God. This love is Spinoza's religion, and its reward is beatitude. It is that state of faith which comes after complete understanding. This religion is also a modern necessity.

Spinoza works with reason but his reason also walks its way towards intuition and in this walking and striving integrally embodies intuition and love. As Das helps us understand it:

> Spinoza has given us his three orders of knowledge, the one excelling the other in ascending order or merit. The first stage is that of quick reactions to external stimuli, giving us only inadequate ideas. The second is the life of science and freedom or the stage of reason. The highest reason gives us fortitude and strength of mind. The third ushers in that state, when the mind

> can perceive immediately. Our instincts become intuition and emotion becomes action. Intuition is not discursive, that is, going from part to part, but it follows from the wholeness of nature. And this stage brings us to *amor Dei* [love of God] It is the consequence of complete self-knowledge, not of all knowledge.

This reason of Spinoza as it strives to realize intuition resonates with supramental reason of Sri Aurobindo and has the potential to heal the pathology of both reason and religion which afflict us today. It also helps us overcome the pathology of anthropocentrism and sociocentrism where man and society become arrogant and establish regimes of control.

In this book on Spinoza Das presents Spinoza's path of understanding God, Nature and Human in the following way: "God is not separate from the world of matter and thought, only ruling it from His high pedestal. He is the world of both matter and thought; he is no where if not in this world." Das has also been a life-long student of Sri Aurobindo and in interpreting Sri Aurobindo's vision Das tells us that for Sri Aurobido, God did not create the world, He became the world (Das 2001). It would be enriching if Das were to engage with Spinoza and Sri Aurobindo together and explore further the resonance between Spinoza's seeking and Sri Aurobindo's yoga especially between Sri Aurobinbo's supramental mode and Spinoza's mode of intuition.[8] As readers let us pray a long life for Das and look forward to such a gift from him.

Das writes the following towards the end of this book:

> Our inventions of power have recoiled upon us in the form of dreadful wars and killings. Our unending additions to the amenities of life bring us everything but happiness. Our mind has been a victim to abnormality, there is disease and decay all around, there is mutual ill-feeling and hatred in all our walks in society. And what is the way out of all this dirt and dross? How can we learn the art of being men? By being more human. By tolerance, by understanding, by accepting the whole world of existence. By coming together, meeting together and working together.[9] More and still more understanding is the imperative way out, it is the yearning need of our time. And all these words we have come across in the vocabulary of Spinoza.

For Das, Spinoza did not judge but tried to understand; despite being excommunicated he loved society and humanity and strove for healing our distorted understanding. And this is the perennial significance of Spinoza as he urges us to realize:

> Rejection reduces man to the chrysalis cave of the Diogenian type of individualism; politically to his own interested group, and in morals, to his pet dogmas. The excellence, in the eyes of the modern age, lies in assimilation and acceptance, accepting the whole of existence as it is. And Spinoza lives eternally as a minister of this spirit of reconciliation.

A recent work on Spinoza presents him as a New Moses who invites us to realize the covenant that God has written with all us, not just Hebraic people, "not with ink and on stone tablets but on the contrary with the spirit of God on the Heart" (Bagley 2008: 242). In this book Das concludes by inviting us to realize Spinoza as an European Krishna striving to combine *Gyana*, *Karma* and *Bhakti*—knowledge, action and devotion. Our present time calls for all of us to strive to embody a New Moses and a New Krishna in our paths of thinking and living. But for this we have to be become a New Mary, a New Yashoda, a Divine Mother, which gives birth to immanence and transcendence, the moment and the eternal, the one and the many, and the infinite and embrace of the One at the same time. Let us hope that this soul-touching work will help us in this epochal and eternal calling of creative mothering.

Bishuba Sankranti
April 14, 2009

Ananta Kumar Giri
Madras Institute of Development Studies
Chennai

REFERENCES

Bagley, Paul J. 2008. *Philosophy, Theology, and Politics: A Reading of Benedict Spinoza's Tractus Theologicus-Politicus*. Leiden: Brill.

Bhaskar, Roy. 2002. *Reflections on Meta-Reality: Transcendence, Everyday Life and Emancipations*, New Delhi: Sage Publication.

Borges, Jose Louis. 1999. *Selected Poems*. London: Penguin.

Das, Chitta Ranjan. 2001. "Integral Education: The Vision and An Experiment." In *Rethinking Social Transformation: Criticism and Creativity at the Turn of the Millennium*, (ed.). Ananta Kumar Giri. Jaipur: Rawat Publications.

2007a *Nakha Darpanenana*. Bhubaneswar: Pathika Prakashani.

2007b. *Kristen Kold: A Revolutionary in Education and the Pioneer of the Danish Folk High School Movement*. Delhi: Shipra Publications.

2009 "Afterword." *The Modern Prince and the Modern Sage: Transforming Power and Freedom*, (ed.), Ananta Kumar Giri. Delhi: Sage Publications.

Erlman, Veit. 1999. *Music, Modernity and the Global Imagination: South Africa and the World*. NY: Oxford U. Press.

Giri, Ananta Kumar. 2008. *Self-Development and Social Transformations? The Vision and the Practice of the Self-Study Mobilization of Swadhyaya*. Jaipur: Rawat.

Habermas, Jurgen. 2003. "Faith and Knowledge." In idem, *The Future of Human Nature*, pp. 101-115. Cambridge: Polity Press.

Heidegger, Martin. 2004. "The End of Philosophy and the Task of Thinking." In idem, *Basic Writings of Martin Heidegger*, pp. 428-449. London: Routledge.

Naess, Arne. *Det frie menneske* (The Free Human Being). Oslo

Nemoianu, Virgil. 2006. "The Church and the Secular Establishment: A Philosophical Dialog Between Joseph Ratzinger and Jurgen Habermas." *Logos* 9 (2): 17-42.

Spinoza, Benedict. 2001. *Ethics*. Hertfordshire: Wordsworth Editions.

ENDNOTES

1. Here what Das writes is helpful to understand what Einstein might have meant with such a statement:

   > What is the God of Spinoza? It is Nature, the external order of essence and existence of things. So when we realize that all our affects follow from the eternal necessity of the order of things, we sense the vastness of this order; in other words, we know God. And as all adequate knowledge leads not to sorrow, but joy, to understand God is to love God. This love is of no utilitarian character; nay, it emanates from the love of knowledge and the joy of liberty, resulting from finding oneself in an ineffaceable order.

2. As Das helps us realize which our fellow readers can look forward to

   > Spinoza, by his union with all by conceiving them under eternity comes very near to the Eastern thought. Knowing things *sub specie aeternitatis*, man knows himself to be in God and God to be in Himself. He becomes a God. Indian philosophy also tells us the same thing. Knowing God and his eternal laws, we also know ourselves as God. *Brahmabid brahmaiba bhabati* — The knower of Brahma becomes Brahma himself-- says the Màndukya. To live *sub specie aeternitatis* can be compared with what Buddha called *Brahma Vihàra* or living, moving and having one's joy in *Brahma*.

3. A book in Oriya which is a collection of his writings; the title of the book refers to the theme of nails and mirrors. Cf. Das 2007a.
4. Most of these books are in Oriya though Das knows and writes in many languages such as Sanskrit, Bengali, Hindi, English, German, Danish and Finnish. His book on Kristen Kold, the pioneer of Danish folk high school movement, originally written in Oriya, has been published in English which in fact is the first book in this book series of ours from Shipra. See Das 2007b.
5. In the same paragraph Das also refers to Sri Aurobindo: "To Sri Aurobindo, a higher consciousness, as a rule, has to prove itself in the world. It never runs away and can afford itself to prove itself to be an asset of the world."
6. This was held at the Catholic Academy of Bavaria, Munich on Jan 19, 2004. See Nemoianu 2006.
7. Ratzinger urges us to realize the significance of bringing reason to religion as do many contemporary socio-religious movements such as the self-study movement of Swadhyaya emanating from Hinduism (see Giri 2008).
8. Among contemporary philosophers Das would also find affinity between Spinoza and Roy Bhaskar who takes his engagement with realism to a new height and depth when he writes:

   The critique of postmodernism involves accepting the emphasis on uniqueness and differentiation without throwing out our concepts of universality and connection. Indeed the ground-state and cosmic envelope are just precisely the concepts we need to understand differentiation within a unity. But these aspects of being, on which all other aspects ultimately depend, are precisely those which through the generalized theory of co-presence, allows us to see that everything is implicitly enfolded or contained and may be brought to consciousness, implicit or explicit, in everything else, so that anything can be traced or manifest in anything else. The world becomes one in which a quasi-magical or generalized (dialectically universalized) synchronicity is potentially capable of being manifest anywhere (Bhaskar 2002: 248).
9. Some weeks ago (In November 2008) while being on the road of life I was walking in the library of University of Manheim, Germany with a dear friend and encountered a book entitled *Music, Modernity and the Global Imagination*. I sat down to take note from the epilogue of the book thoughtfully entitled, "The Art of the Impossible." What I read resonates with the spirit of Spinoza and Das as it also presents us the insights of another contemporary thinker Peter Sloterdijk from Germany:

   > [For Sloterdijk], all known forms of politics have consisted in the art of the possible, in the ability to conceive of the widest possible community—primal horde, tribe, nation—and to ensure its manipulation through the successful manipulation of all inclusive, collective imaginations and autohypnoses. [But the price we pay for this is too high] In the age of the hyperpolitics everything reaches a point of no return, and, ultimately, human beings without return. And so,

> Sloterdijk concludes, in the age of "last" people it is time to reconsider smaller forms of association in which man must learn anew the oldest art, that of reproducing man through man (Erlman 1999: 281).

This art of reproducing man through man though mutuality, friendship and yoga resonates with the strivings of Chitta Ranjan Das who in his recent works challenges us to go beyond a gendered and biological view of reproduction and all of us be creative mothers. Das also challenges us to adorn our mind and modes of thinking with feminine beauty which possibly is a creative advance over Spinoza's mode of thinking as Spinoza had doubt about the capacity for "intellectual love for God" on the part of women. But the author of the book Erlman thinks that we can not just go back to smaller forms of association which he calls "paleo-politics" (ibid). He writes: "[We cannot return] to a new paleo-politics [cannot reduce complexity to simplicity [..] but explore the rudiments of a future politics and cultural practice as the art of the impossible." We can also look at the strivings of Benedict Spinoza and Chitta Ranjan Das as an art of the impossible in thinking and practice.

Preface

Several years back, in my early twenties, when I was a student of philosophy in the renowned poet Rabindra Nath Thakur's International Seat of Learning at Santiniketan, India, I was called upon to write a dissertation as a part of my final examination, I chose Spinoza.

But my teachers had hesitations about it. They told me that neither of them, had any specific acquaintance with Baruch Spinoza's contribution to philosophy and therefore could not help me in my job as guides. Neither had I; yet I stuck to Spinoza and wrote the dissertation. There were many who helped, especially our Librarian who got me the needed literature from libraries, from around the world, with our university bearing the cost.

That happened in 1948. Meanwhile, my interests have spilled out to many other life-directions and understandably, I have not really done any further academic study of Spinoza. Many serious students must have discovered Spinoza in newer lights and dimensions. I must admit that I have not been in touch.

Nevertheless, Spinoza has always remained with me, and enriched me, helped me to understand more and more completely, understand with love and willing involvement. It is very heartening to see that active thinkers and doers from almost all disciplines and human concerns find Spinoza so relevant.

I was not sure about the worth of bringing out in print my dissertation, which I had written long ago. I am grateful to Dr. Ananta Kumar Giri for his persistence without which I would not have sent my work for publication.

If one will, one may always take this introduction as an apology as well.

Bishuba Sankranti
April 14, 2009

CHITTA RANJAN DAS
83/A, Bapuji Nagar
Bhubaneswar-751009
email: sikshasandhan@gmail.com

Content

Foreword v

Preface xvii

1. Introduction **1**
A Life Sketch 1
Spinoza's Works 9
The Background of Spinoza's Philosophy 12

2. Spinoza: Stated and Restated **20**
The Spinozistic Approach 20
The Method Geometrico 25
Substance, Attributes and Modes 31
The Human Mind 41
This Human Nature 50
The Man in Bondage 58
Deliverance of Man 70
Spinoza and Theology 85
On Polity and Politics 92

3. Spinoza Through the Ages **100**

4. Spinoza Reconsidered **115**

5, The Man and His Philosophy **150**

6. The Eternal Spinoza **154**

1

Introduction

A mighty oak here ruined lies
Its top was wont to kiss the skies
Why is it now overthrown?-
The peasants needed, so they said,
Its wood wherewith to build a shed
And so they have cut it down.

—A Poem by Schiller

A Life Sketch

"By the sentence of the angels, by the decree of the saints, we anathemize, cut off, curse and execrate Baruch Spinoza, in the presence of these sacred books, with the six hundred and thirteen precepts which are written therein [...] with all the cursings which are written in the book of the Law; cursed be he by day and cursed by night, cursed when he lieth down and cursed when he riseth up, cursed when he goeth out and cursed when cometh in; the Lord pardon him never, the wrath and fury of the Lord burn upon this man and bring upon him all the curses which are written in the book of the Law. The Lord blot out his name under heaven. The Lord set him apart from destruction from all the tribes of Israel with all the curses of the firmament which are written in the book of the Law [...] There shall be no man [to] speak to him, no man [to] write to him, no man show him any kindness, no man stay under the same roof with him, no man come nigh him."

With these solemn words, the Rabbi Fathers of the Jewish Synagogue at Amsterdam had excommunicated Baruch de Spinoza, then only a young man of twenty-four.

This was the only way open before them to get rid of this insubordinate youngster, who showed conclusive signs of going against the established faith.

But when Baruch was a boy at school, the learned Fathers had highly admired his talent and granted him scholarship. "He will be a pride to our race," the teachers used to remark, "and as learned and acute a Rabbi as ever our people did produce."

Baruch was born on November 24, 1632, of well-to-do Jewish parents. His forefathers had emigrated from Spain to escape the horrors of the Inquisition. Those fugitives had settled in the Netherlands, the newly-formed Republic which declared that every citizen, should remain free in his religion and that no man should be molested or questioned on the subject of divine worship!

The Jews, in course of time, had been granted a Synagogue of their own but were not given full freedom in religion and worship. They were still foreigners, and had to guard the members of their own faith against going astray and bringing persecution to the race.

Spinoza's early training was carried within the faithful bounds of the Jewish texts. From the very beginning, he showed extraordinary brilliance at school. Though his inclination was towards commerce, his father picked him for Rabbinical education. Under Morteira, he mastered the Hebrew language and literature and finished the Old Testament and the Talmud. The precocity of his intellect brought him in the good books of the elders. But gradually, Spinoza's scholarly inquisitiveness brewed into undaunted inquiries about various subjects and questions which often bewildered him.

With an intention to clarify his doubts, Spinoza made a minute study of the Hebraic Scriptures but the deeper he dived, the more inquisitive he became. The scope of study was too limited. Greek and Latin had no place in it. Spinoza's enthusiasm must have been very intense to study the latter, the one vehicle through which the deeper philosophical thoughts of the time were recorded! Within the Synagogue, there was also a religious spite for Classical studies, as the 'foster-mother of heathen admirations', and one of Spinoza's school-fellows, 'looked back upon the acquisition of Latin as a sin and imposed upon himself a forty days' fast to wash the language from his memory and the stain from his conscience.'

The inquiry into the meaning of the Scriptures gave rise to many doubts in Spinoza's mind and made him suspicious of them. He aspired for a free flight into the truth of things and moulded independent opinions for himself, even at the risk of offending the current interpretations. Once, when asked certain questions by two of his school-mates, he gave certain 'heretical' opinions. These, the faithless companions reported to the authorities of the Synagogue, who, irritated at his impertinence, summoned him for an explanation. The charge against him was that 'he had derided the Jews as ignorant of physics and theology and praised their law as a piece of adroit management of unruly men.' Spinoza obeyed the orders with 'gay carelessness' but could not be persuaded to go back on the views he had already professed. Morteira tried his best to bring his pupil to path but finding him incorrigible, angrily dissolved the assembly and vowed 'only to return with the thunderbolt in his hand.'

All this storm and fire of the fanatic elders had little effect on Spinoza's intellectual passion. To study Latin, the language of philosophy, was his only purpose in mind. Descartes was the center of discussion on philosophical problems in contemporary Europe. From all platforms, hot and enthusiastic debates centered round the problems, which had been raised by Descartes. The passport to learned circles thus presupposed a thorough knowledge of Descartes. And his two great works, *The Meditations* and *The Principia*, were written in Latin. To understand Descartes, then, necessitated being well-versed in Latin.

While Spinoza was looking for a teacher who could teach him Latin, he came in contact with Van den Ende, a Catholic physician and Latin master by profession. Van den Ende had a bad name among the Jews as a free thinker; a man, who upheld the radical views and taught the 'Latin wisdom which carried in it not only the heathen thought of past ages but also the rising sciences and the philosophy of the present, Spinoza made arrangements for learning Latin with Van den Ende as a resident usher in the master's house. Under this free atmosphere and a free thinking man, Spinoza found the right environment he was in search of. This association was an important event in his mental development and in the birth of the philosopher. Van den Ende himself had been a victim of the Dutch Protestants for his frank allegiance to reason and repudiation of theology. It was but natural that one wild bird could be at home with another elder one.

Biographers refer here to a love affair of Spinoza, the only one of its kind, with Clara Ende, the daughter of his master. She was a bright girl and was entrusted with teaching Latin to Spinoza. It was not very unnatural that the pupil and the teacher were mutually attracted and Spinoza fell in love with the girl. But before the love could ripen to a union, the girl was married to Kerckkrinck, a fellow scholar of Spinoza, who won the bargain and 'easily cut out the olive-faced philosopher by the bribe of a pearl necklace and a good address.' This was too long a pursuit for Spinoza to go farther in the affair and he returned to philosophy and never again dangled after any woman.

It was not long before Spinoza could have a good grasp over Latin and soon poured himself over difficult books. First he studied Divinity, then natural philosophy. He finished the works of Descartes, the prince of all philosophers, with hasty greed. Now he became a versatile linguist. Earlier, he had been well-versed in Hebrew, German, Italian, Spanish, Portuguese and Dutch, and now Latin was added to the long list.

But the more he grew in wisdom, the more grew the rage of the Synagogue. His obstinacy of philosophical pursuits became a regular worry for the fathers of the tribe and kept them concerned about it. They saw in this solitary truth seeker, a breaker of creeds and conventional beliefs, a man who was a danger to the solidarity of the race. Moreover, Spinoza's association with Francis Ende, that God-denying materialist, who taught atheism side by side with Latin, prompted the authorities to take a hasty step to bring down the young tartar. The primary methods were naturally those of appeasement. A prize gift of 1000 florins annually was promised to him if only he desisted from doubting the established faith. The offer failed. More drastic measures were soon to follow. The Synagogue issued on him a decree of ecclesiastical censure for thirty days. During this time, an attempt at stabbing him to death was made by an intolerant zealot. Fortunately, the young philosopher escaped the blow only with his mantle pierced.

The thirty days were over but Spinoza was as adamant as ever. Many attempts were made to silence him but he retorted with equal scorn and carelessness. So the last verdict came on 27th July 1656, when he was formally excommunicated from the Synagogue. It was Morteira, once his friend and teacher, who ordered the execution of the sentence amidst a huge gathering of faithful Jews who had come to see the heretic being delivered his due.

Spinoza welcomed the proclamation with his usual poise of mind. On receiving the news, he is said to have remarked, "This compels me to nothing which I should not otherwise have done." He had written a long reply to the tribal fathers but the letter still remains untraced. To commemorate the occasion, he changed the initial of his name from Baruch to the Latin word Benedict, meaning blessed.

Spinoza was only twenty-four then, unaware of what was in store for him. He had been left alone to cover the rest of the long tedious journey.

Spinoza then shifted to Ouwerkerk Road, in the vicinity of Amsterdam, and lived with one of his acquaintances, in a place quite near to his collegiate friends. There he was able to earn his humble penny by polishing glasses for microscopes and telescopes etc. The laws in the sacred book, *Ethic of the Fathers* advised every Jew to learn some mechanical art. It was not enough to be a scholar, the means of subsistence must also be learned. Thus, Spinoza had already learnt the art while in the Synagogue.

He sent the polished lenses to the town which his friends sold in the market and sent the money to Spinoza. Through this art, Spinoza could also gather much knowledge in physical science and soon earned reputation as an expert in optics. It was as an experimenter in optics that he came in contact with many important men of the line, like Oldenburg, Bole and Leibnitz. He also wrote a *Treatise on Rainbow*, a discourse on some physical problems. His favourite pastime was drawing and he made some portraits of men with chalk and charcoal. His time in Ouwerkerk was mostly spent in attentive study and in condensation of some of his original ideas. This was the time of severe vacillations of his mind. The storm was certainly the birth-pangs which preceded the advent of the full-fledged philosopher.

As Spinoza enriched himself in wisdom, the rich men at Amsterdam gave serious thoughts to get rid of him. Even Cartesianism, which Spinoza was alleged to be frequently discussing, was looked down by them with suspicion. And the Cartesians also wanted to keep clean of Spinoza by occasional invectives against him, so that they might not also be denounced as heretics. All these troubles led Spinoza to retire to the village of Rejnsburg near Leyden. He had turned twenty eight. The solitary village environment fitted very much with his inclinations of mind and he could devote most of his time to serious studies.[1] Next year, again, he shifted to Voorburg, a hamlet near The Hague. He was being already discussed as an original thinker and philosopher. During this period also, he came across many distinguished men, including high-ranking government officers like Jane de Witt. This same man, De Witt was later killed by an angry mob at The Hague.

Spinoza had a circle of disciples at The Hague, who were taking philosophical guidance from his letters and manuscripts sent to them through private arrangement. These disciples, many of them very prominent in the affairs of the state, requested Spinoza to come to live in the town. This led Spinoza to move to The Hague in 1670 where he stayed till his death.

At The Hague, a modestly equipped house, well suited for his simple living was rented out for Spinoza. But the cost of living there being too high, Spinoza shifted to another house where he stayed with the family of a painter, Van den Spijck by name. Three important incidents happened during these years. The first was the cruel and cold blooded murder of De Witt by the enraged people of The Hague. Though Spinoza 'habitually looked at the storms of human life from a cold and quiet height,' this murder of a good man, so well known to him, stirred up his sentiments. With eyes brimming with angry tears, he resolved to condemn the criminal act at the very place of murder and prepared a handbill to be pasted up for this purpose. This could not materialize, however, as the host had already taken precautions in locking the house-door and refusing exit.

The second was Col. Stoupe's invitation to him on behalf of General Conde. The French, before attacking Holland, had been stationed at Utrecht. Spinoza, with his usual simplicity, complied with the request and went there. Stoupe welcomed the philosopher and expressed the intention of Conde to grant him a pension, provided he dedicated a book of his to the French King. By nature, Spinoza was high above these bargains. He thankfully refused the offer and came back to The Hague. But during his absence, an angry crowd had gathered before his house. It had harboured suspicions behind

1. At Rejnsburg the Spinoza Lane is still there and there still stands the house he lived in. The house is now called the Spinoza Huis or Spinoza Museum.

Spinoza's motive in paying a visit to the invader's camp. The host was afraid of the rioters who wanted to break into the house and drag out the enemy-agent. "Fear nothing", replied Spinoza, "it is for me to justify myself and there are persons enough who know the object of my journey; but whatever may arrive, as soon as the people assemble before your door, I will go out and meet them, even if they should do to me what they did to the good De Witts." And he perorated, "I am a good republican and have never had anything in view but the good and glory of the State." Fortunately, the turmoil subsided peacefully and the people, convinced, dispersed at last leaving the philosopher to his studies.

The last was the offer to 'the very acute and renowned philosopher Benedict de Spinoza' of a professorship in philosophy in the University of Heidelberg. It was made by Karl Ludwig, the then Elector Palatine. This invitation kept no restriction on the professor's right of philosophizing but believed that 'he would not use this freedom for disturbing the religion publicly established.' But Spinoza had never harboured the ambition of giving public instruction. And being faithful to his lonely pursuit of truth, a worthier necessity for him, he declined the offer. "I can not be induced to embrace this glorious opportunity," he wrote, "although I have debated the matter with myself for a long time." Perhaps, the instruction of young men would have been an obstacle to his own studies and diverted his mind to other things. This reminds one of Chuang Tzu, the Chinese scholar-sage of 300 B.C. who once declined a premiership in favour of free thought and peace.

In the year 1673, Spinoza had turned forty one. But the overwork and long hours of strenuous study had already ruined his health. And while polishing his lenses, he was gradually developing consumption.[2] The premature death came very peacefully on 21st February, 1677, when the host and his family were away for prayer. Thus ended the life of a philosopher who was anathemized by his society, disowned by the learned men of the age, only to be resuscitated in the future years.

Apart from his philosophy, Spinoza's life itself was remarkable and great. Surrounded by a hostile community, with persecuting

---

2. It means symptoms of tuberculosis.

threats equally from the Jewry and the Gentile, he sailed solemnly his lonely boat and never cursed the world for being unkind to him.

He lived a very simple life. His wants were but few and so also his possessions. His inventory consisted of not more than sixty volumes. After his death, it was found that, apart from his unpublished manuscripts, he had left nothing but a row of books, a few lenses, a simple bed and clothings. His clean and unsophisticated living can be clear from the account left by Colerus, his first biographer. "He was very sober and frugal all the time. Not that he was reduced to so great a poverty as not to be able to spend more, if he had been willing; he had friends enough who offered him their purses. But he was naturally very sober and was satisfied with little. He lived a whole day upon a milk soup done with butter which cost 3 and upon a pot of beer of 3½ d. Another day he ate nothing but gruel done with raisin and butter which cost him 4½ d. Though he was often invited to eat with his friends he chose rather to live upon what he had at home, than to sit down at a good table at the expense of another man." Again "he was careful to cast up his accounts every quarter, he lived from hand to mouth. He compared himself to the serpent who forms a circle with his tail in his mouth, meaning that he saved nothing."

His aversion for having more than what was necessary was magnanimous. One of his friends and admirers, Simon de Vries wanted to leave his whole property to Spinoza which the latter declined in favour of the former's brother, the rightful owner of the property. Even the annual 500 florins, de Vries had left for him, he would accept only 300, as was only necessary. A second incident occurred; after his father's death, his sister wanted to deprive him of all property. Spinoza appealed to law against this illegal encroachment upon his right, had it vindicated by winning the case, but then gave his actual share to his sister and only kept a bed for him to sleep on.

About his bodily appearance and ways of life, Colerus writes: "He was medium-sized, had good facial features, black skinned, he was very careless of his dress. Once about it, Spinoza remarked that a good man was never the better for having a finer gown. It is unreasonable to wrap up things of little or no value in a precious cover."

His manners and conversations were remarkable. Most of his time he spent inside his chamber. If tired he walked downstairs, talked to the members of the house, or smoked a pipe. He took a childlike interest in making the spiders fight, or in throwing a fly into the cobweb and often, in himself, burst into laughter.

He was very catholic in his religious beliefs. His faith and ideas on theology did never infringe upon those of others. He even attended the sermons if they were from a sincere preacher. Once when his landlady asked him whether she could be saved in the religion she professed, Spinoza replied, "Your religion is a good one, you need not look for another, nor doubt that you may be saved in it, provided, whilst you apply yourself to piety, you live at the same time a peaceable and quiet life." His letter to the Elector Palatine also bears the same spirit; "Religious quarrels do not arise so much from an ardent zeal for religion as from men's various dispositions, and the love of contradiction which makes them habitually distort and condemn everything." How similarly it reads with Mahatma Gandhi's remark, "Difference of opinion does not mean dissension. Unity in diversity is nature's law. It is egotism which is the divisive force."[3]

Spinoza's Works

Toynbee, in his *Study of History* speaks of a period of 'withdrawal and return' in the lives of heroes of history and leaders of thought. The assertion has much truth in it. Mahatma Gandhi was first a lonely experimenter in South Africa before he came to India. Lenin had for many years kept himself away from the political happenings in Tsarist Russia. Machiavelli, the prince-maker, owes much for his greatness as a political thinker, to his long term incarceration. Whitby, in his *Makers of Man,* theorizes that, to the ethico-religious innovator, solitude is a *sine qua non.* 'Guilty', the unconventional thinker feels himself to be in the society of the conforming majority; hence, perforce, during his periods of mental gestation, like a woman concealing her shame, he dwells apart, until the burden of his mind acquires substance and form, and is ready for its birth into a hostile and envious world.

---

3. Harijan: 7.7.46.

Spinoza passed through this necessary phase of solitude after his banishment from the Synagogue. Only then could he find the necessary peace and leisure to satisfy his omnivorous appetite for knowledge. The God of Knowledge is a heavy task master, and the road to Him can only be paved by one who is worthy of it.

At Ouwerkerk, Spinoza lived with his Collegiant friends. His first philosophical work was a *Short Treatise on God, Man and His Well-Being* (Discovered in 1862). It is a fragmentary work clearly showing the mental undulations of Spinoza during his busiest years of study. This maiden work, Martinue says, is 'the first landing place of his mind in his independent advance.[4] This was only an experimental theme of an unripe mind.

His two years at Rejnsburg were probably among the most fruitful in his mental history. Korthott says of those days that "he devoted himself to studies far into the night, and for the most part toiled by lamplight from the tenth evening hour until the third."[5] He devoted his days to the making of lenses. He rarely came out of his study room. Once he shut himself for a period of three months. Time and space were nothing to this wizard of knowledge, who lived in and for eternity. This was also the case with many who have lived for philosophy. Descartes did not come out of his room for a whole day and shut himself there before he had mapped out a scheme of his life work. Newton often forgot his meals, Hegel once left a shoe in the mud without being conscious of the loss.

In 1663 Spinoza brought out the *Abridgement of the Meditations of Descartes* in two volumes, with an Appendix, the *Cogitata Metaphysica* bearing his own annotations and critical remarks. This was the only book which saw the light during Spinoza's lifetime with the author's name printed on it.

Next, he simultaneous worked upon two books, *De Intellectus Emendartione* and the *Ethic*. The former was his reaction after reading Descartes's *Discours de la Methode* and Bacon's *Novum Organon*. It can be called Spinoza's 'spiritual autobiography' or his 'Organon'. "It is an analytical introduction to the consecutive

---

4. Martinue's, p. 35.
5. Wolf's, p. 391.

exposition of his system, which he [..] essayed in *The Ethic*."[6] Unfortunately this first book remained unfinished and the second, which took him four years, *The Ethic*, could only be published after his death.

During his stay at Voorburg, Spinoza was working on developing *The Ethic*, and also completing another book on politics and theology. The latter was the *Tractatus Theologicus Politicus*. In a letter, from Voorburg, Spinoza stated the reasons for writing the book as follows: (1) The prejudices of theologians: for I know that these are among the chief obstacles which prevent men from directing their mind to philosophy; and so I do all I can to expose them and to remove them from the minds of the more prudent. (2) The opinion which the common people have of me, who do not cease to accuse me falsely of atheism, I am also obliged to avert this accusation as far as possible, and (3) The freedom of philosophizing and of saying what we think, this I desire to vindicate in every way, for here it is always suppressed through the excessive authority and impudence of the preachers."[7]

This treatise, when it came out in 1669, incurred the wrath of the authorities no sooner than it saw the light. It was denounced as a wicked book 'forged in hell by a renegade Jew and the Devil.' Though anonymously published, it soon became an open secret that Spinoza was its author.

The 17th Century in Europe, Windelband writes, was an era of 'strife of methods'. The dawn of scientific reasoning greatly encouraged thinking men to give out their own solutions to problems. But the authorities could not brook these new endeavours and became notorious for arresting a free growth of thought. The state had become only a protege of the church. People had not forgotten the horrible days of the Spanish Inquisition and the regime of Bloody Mary in England. The church dreaded the advance of scientific ideas which led men to reason out everything they had been taught till then to believe. The entire European populace saw Copernicus and Galileo succumb to the iron hands of the state, Giordano Bruno's hylozoistic pantheism conflicted violently with the anthropomorphic God of the scriptures and he was burnt at the heretic's stake. All this had warned

---

6. Encyclopaedia Britannica—under CARTESIANISM.
7. Letter no. 30.

the philosophers to be cautious in giving out what they thought. Descartes had to burn his work on cosmology, *De Mundi*, when he heard the sad end of Bruno. Spinoza realized the pulse of the age and wisely published *Tractatus Theologico-Politicus* only anonymously, 'to avoid the risk of odium and persecution.' And it is known from one of his letters that after he had made all the arrangements to publish *The Ethic*, he heard the people talking of a book, in the press, which openly disproved the existence of God. Not much hopeful about the reception the book would have from the people, and wisely aware of the dangers that might involve his life, he immediately gave up the project of printing the book and started writing his *Tractatus Theologicus Politicus* which he left unfinished. It was only after his death that his unpublished works were published in 1677 with the title of *Opera Posthuma*. It contained *The Ethic*, *Tractatus Politicus*, (unfinished), *De Intellects Emendatione* (unfinished) and a short treatise on Hebrew grammar. Another work of his, which has been traced out as late as 1915 is the *Tractatus Bellico-Pacifique*, enunciating his ideas on war and peace.

We also know from Colerus that, in his later days, Spinoza had started a translation of the Old Testament into Dutch, had finished five books of Moss, but burnt them before his death.

The Background of Spinoza's Philosophy

Spinoza's early upbringing was in the midst of Jewish folklore. The Jews at Amsterdam were a docile community yet considering themselves as immigrants from Spain. The Synagogue had its stringent moral code and unquestionable social discipline. The school taught nothing except the Hebrew language and the Books of Israel. Jehovah, the old tribal God, still ruled the popular faith. And in this narrow space for self-expression, Spinoza had no escape.

Spinoza's association with Van den Ende was a notable event in his growth as a philosopher. Here he could freely judge things for himself and could give vent to what he thought. Martinue sums up the effect on Spinoza of this contact in the following lines: "[..] in Van den Ende's house he first drew breath in a scientific atmosphere, and strongly felt both the attractions and perplexities of the ultimate problems of natural knowledge [..] and turning from the spoken thoughts of men in the literature of religion, he tried to read the silent language of the [cosmic] order respecting its own source and essence."[8] His excommunication gave him better scopes for free thought and made him free to weave out his own ideas.

At Ouwerkerk, he read Descartes with due keenness. At Rejnsburg he came very near to the Collegiants--a group of settlers holding liberal religious ideas. Comparing them with the modern Quakers, Martinue writes, "They so held to the Divine Spirit in man as to insist upon dogmatic freedom; they refused to take an oath or serve in war, they allowed any brother spiritually moved, to speak in their assembly, and retained no ritual element in their Christianity. They combined in an unusual degree, an openness of knowledge and love of scientific truth."[9] "To Spinoza, their freedom of mind and simplicity were congenial."[10] But though much influenced by these Collegiants, Spinoza never took to the Christian faith nor became a member in their order.

He gave serious thoughts to the philosophy of Descartes, was mused seriously on his ideas on determinism, method and truth. "In this interval his speculative system was wrought out in its full proportions in his mind, so as to bring ontology, physics, ethics, politics into one organism."[11]

Spinoza's mind was still in a formative state and his treatment of method in the 'short-treatise' indicates that he was only beating about the bush. The Appendix he added to his work on Descartes also came from a premature brain. But one thing was certain that after his first book was published, he came in the lime-light of contemporary thought and was widely recognized as a philosopher of some worth. His correspondence was extended to a big circle of intellectuals also including scientists. While at Voorburg, again he had to give practical lessons to a circle of young aspirants; often he sent his unpublished chapters to be read and debated upon in that circle, got the readers' doubts and criticisms communicated to him and, if necessary, made a revision of the chapters. The corrections and additions in the margins in his manuscripts are a sure proof of this. These examinations and re-

---

8. Martinue's, p. 22.
9. Martinue, Types of Ethical Theory, p. 240.
10. Martinue's, p. 39.
11. *Ibid*, p. 39.

examinations, and above all, reading into the readers' reactions to his philosophical themes before they got their final text, helped much to Spinoza in having a thorough grasp over his own ideas.

Spinoza's correspondence had a long tether extended to manifold regions and interests. Beginning from the puerile belief in ghosts (Boxel wrote to him that he believed in the existence of spirits of all kinds except, possibly female spirits), it also dealt with theology, physics, chemistry and philosophy. And dealing with them made Spinoza acquainted with an extensive field of knowledge. From the seed, which waited looking for an outlet soon evolved the free man, and when Spinoza finished his *Ethic*, he knew with confidence that he was serving out something which was his own.

Again, to quote Toynbee, the great men of thought 'dilate the social soul in themselves.' The man of genius is never a hot house growth. Though he develops himself in society and is subject to the reaction of the society, the vast experience makes him grow and evolve, and still he is not a product of society. He takes the fibres from the world but weaves the robe himself applying his own genius. Historical materialism is wrong when it asserts that the leader or hero is only a replica of the society he lives in. Thus Spinoza cannot be proved to be a mere product of this or that movement of thought. No doubt, he took much from the society but what he gave was cent per cent his own. He was conspicuous by his own approach and to the treatment of the very problems also handled by those who had preceded him.

Spinoza's first philosophical schooling was from the Hebraic Scriptures and the works of the Jewish philosophers. The Bible contains everything but science and humour. Absence of science anticipates a hypothetical treatment of things and thus Judaism starts with God as an a priori. Spinoza also begins with God and in this sense he is a Jew. Like the Talmud, he also upholds the relativity of good and evil. The Kabbalah also has much to account for Spinoza's pantheistic and mystical views. It is written in the Commentary of the Kabbalistic book Zohar that 'the creator is himself at once the knowledge, and that which knows and that which is known… Nothing exists which is not united to him or which he finds not in his own substance!' Maimonides, the Jewish mystic writes that he is the intellect, the intelligent and the intelligible. In a letter to Oldeberg Spinoza also echoes the same idea: "I hold God for the immanent cause of all things, not the transient. All things have their being and move in God."

Chasdai Creskas (1340-1410), the Jewish philosopher comes much near to Spinoza. He proved the existence of God from the impossibility of conceiving a world, entirely conditioned and dependent, without some unconditional ground, some un-caused or self-caused cause to sustain it all. Spinoza took much from this for his theory of substance. He conceived God (or Nature or Substance) not as merely a member in the infinite process but as the unconditional ground or immanent cause which sustains the whole and expresses himself in the whole.[12] The Jewish schools were imbued with Neo-plantonism which is semi-Oriental in character. So Spinoza is shown to have inherited much from the East, even to the extreme, which Melamed goes in proving, that he falls in line with Buddha.[13]

But attempting to prove his similarity will be doing injustice to our philosopher. Though Spinoza adopted his philosophy from diverse sources, still, as Melamed remarks, 'there is a yawning gap between him and the medieval Jewish philosophers.' Many critics, who are quick in typifying philosophy, trace Spinoza's determinism to Creskas, his depersonalization of God and Amor Dei to Maimonides, his doctrine of the Attributes to Saadia and his pantheism to Abraham ibn Ezra. But they forget one essential difference between Spinoza and the others. Judaism teaches of a living God concerned with man while Spinoza identifies God with Nature including all the modes of existence. Spinoza did never aspire to propagate the Jewish religion. He was more anti-Jewish than Jewish. He treated his race often with aversion and hate. "The Rabbis are crazy. The bible commentators are dreamers and inventors of falsehood, and the Kabbalists are jabberers."[14] Nature, to the Jewish elders, was 'sin, lust and desire' and God was 'pure, incorporeal and spiritual'. The first book of the Pentateuch is profuse in its contempt of Nature. 'And God saw the earth, and behold! It was corrupt, for all flesh had corrupted its way upon the earth'.

---

12. Wolfe's, p. 397.
13. Spinoza and Buddha—Univ. of Chicago Press, 1933.
14. Tr. Th. Pol. Ch. IX and X.

During Spinoza's association with the Collegiants, he was a little attracted towards the Christian faith. Spinoza's idea of one substance reads similar to St.Paul's motto. 'In Him we live, move and have our being'. His inclination towards Christianity can account for his changing the initials from Baruch to the Latin 'Benedict'. But in spite of the persuasion from men like Steno, he never cherished the idea of a conversion to that religion.

Spinoza also owes much to Anselem, the Archbishop of Canterbury during the reign of Henry I in England. Anselem assumed that the fact alone that we think of God proves His existence. Another thinker of the medieval times, who had some influence on Spinoza, was Jacob Boehme, to whom God is eternal rest, a stillness without being, causeless and will-less. From Anselem, Spinoza borrowed the ontological method and from Boehme, the doctrine of the God without will and intellect.

The last two but the most important men of European thought to whom Spinoza devoted serious thought and, in fact, through whom he entered the world of philosophy were Bruno and Descartes. Most likely, Spinoza adopted the words 'attribute' and 'mode' from Bruno though giving them different significations. Spinoza's highest kind of love, the intellectual love of God, can also be faintly traced in Bruno.

Spinoza's first sailing through philosophy was through Cartesianism. The frank and unreserved way in which Descartes had stated his ideas allured this young truth-seeker. In fact, Descartes is recognized as the father of modern philosophy. With his discourse on Method, the world was acquainted with a new approach to ultimate questions. With him, philosophy was brought down from the realm of anthropomorphic theology to rationalism. Revelation gave way to reason. Descartes started as a mathematician, he also tried to give a scientific explanation to the universal problems and 'to combine the results in a consistent whole'. 'Cogito ergo sum' was his basic principle. Because I think, *ipso facto*, I am. The first of the four rules of this method was, 'Never to accept anything for true which I did not clearly know to be such, that is to say, carefully to avoid precipitancy and prejudice and to compromise nothing more in my judgement than what was presented to my mind so clearly and distinctly as to exclude all grounds of doubt'. This puritan 'no' to all prejudices and presumptions ushered in a new fervor to the thinking of the age. The spirit of Descartes's treatment appealed most to Spinoza and he studied it with the utmost empathy. He prepared exhaustive notes on the various problems of Cartesianism for his private pupils. According to Lewes, 'Descartes captivated him by the boldness of his logic and by the independent nature of his Method, whereby truth was sought in the inner world of man, not in the outer world, nor in the records of authority.'[15]

Because of his close attachment to Descartes, Spinoza is said by many critics to have only improved upon the former's ideas. As Leibnitz remarked in a letter, after his acquaintance with all of Spinoza's writings, 'We may say that Spinoza has only developed certain seeds of Descartes's philosophy'. Some even say that Spinozism was but the logical outcome of Cartesianism and whoever had entrusted himself with the task must have arrived at the same conclusions as Spinoza did. This is giving too long a rope to the process of give and take in philosophy. Spinoza was never a disciple of Descartes, he hardly came near to the Cartesians as will be clear from the succeeding chapters. He had started with Descartes; by studying him he could enunciate his own doubts regarding the order of things, and his work only repudiated the Cartesian doctrine.

Descartes's philosophy began with the premise, 'I think, therefore I am'. From his own mind, Descartes had proceeded to his own body and then to the universal mind or God. Spinoza's doubt began with his bringing in the universal mind from one's own mind. 'Cogito, ergo sum', to Spinoza, was irreproachable, but how, from this could follow 'Cogito, ergo Deus est'? (I think, therefore God is) what was the casual connection that interlinks the two? From this original doubt, Spinoza attempted to give his own solutions.

Spinoza could be convinced of Descartes's arguments that (a) the basis of all certitude was consciousness, (b) whatever is perceived clearly in consciousness is necessarily true. Distinct ideas are the true ideas. (c) Metaphysical problems are susceptible to mathematical demonstration. In this last assertion of Descartes was the first germination of Spinoza. Thinking on its practical application, Spinoza could visualize a vast structural order which could eliminate all doubts and problems. Spinoza's novelty was in applying this method to philosophy. Again quoting from Lewes's book, "This [applying the

---

15. Lewes, Biographical History of Philosophy, p. 395.

new method] may seem a trifling addition, in reality it was the source of all the differences between Spinoza and his teacher."[16]

Spinoza also theorized on state and citizenship. He wrote two books on politics. It is well known that the ground of his political thought was prepared after a scholarly reading of Hobbes. Hobbes's book *De Cive* was printed in Holland in 1647. Spinoza's treatment of the forms of government smacks of an indebtedness to Machiavelli, the Prince-maker. Melamed writes that, epistemologically viewed, Spinoza fully adheres, not to Descartes, but to Hobbes. His theory of genetic definitions he borrowed from Hobbes, just as from Bacon, he took the terms *Natura Naturans* and *Natura Naturata.*

When judging a philosopher and pressing labels on his philosophy, we must not forget the historical aspect of a movement of thought. Spinoza should, therefore, be viewed against the background of the contemporary Jewish society as well as of the attitude of the existing society to philosophy in general. As Pollock writes in his masterly book on Spinoza, the Jews, at Spinoza's time had great scholarship but little sound thinking. The society was rotting in age-long superstitions and preposterous theologies. Demoniacs, exorcisms, miracles, false prophets and even false messiahs fed the credulity of the Levantine Jews. People had a keen interest in reading religious texts but shuddered at any new idea which interfered with the old faith. Free thinkers were branded as infidels and were mercilessly dealt with even worse than criminals. Fifteen years before Spinoza's excommunication, Uriel Da Costa had also been outlawed for seven years for revolting against the Rabbinical gloss and tradition. The same reign of iron rod prevailed in the entire continent. Every good citizen was supposed to not question the authenticity of sacred scriptures. All new opinions on science and religion were censured with primitive cruelty. Most men thought themselves learned if only they knew. But they never stepped to reason out what they knew. Crass intellectualism was the order of the day and the people did not want anything more. Looking upon this historical background, Melamed says in the introductory chapter of his book, Spinozism was a necessary phenomenon in the 17th century in Europe as was Christianity in its time.

---

16. *Ibid*, p. 397.

'Words deceive us as girls do',[17] remarked Romain Rolland. He had also warned us not to be confounded in the maze that the words spread around us. 'The ill use of words', he observed, 'results in errors and obscurity, mistakes and confusion [..] There is some reason to doubt whether language, as it has been employed, has contributed more to the improvement or hindrance of knowledge amongst mankind.' By misunderstanding particular words, we are often prone to misinterpret a philosopher who uses them. And Spinoza no less escapes this misunderstanding. The 17th century in Europe was the time when scholastic discussions over terms like substance, attribute, mode, essence, existence and eternity were in the air. These terms were already in vogue before Spinoza. Spinoza used each of these terms, though with varied colours and implications. This is mainly where critics are pitifully confused. They read Spinoza's work through other men's interpretations and make his elucidations difficult for comprehension.

17. Romain Rolland, I will not Rest. p. 61.

2

Spinoza: Stated and Restated

> We never read a book. We read ourselves through books either to discover ourselves or guide ourselves. The greatest book is not that whose contents are imprinted upon the brain as a telegraphic message is recorded on a strip of paper, but that whose vital shock awakens other existences, spreading from one to another the fire which feeds upon diverse resources, until, assuming the proportions of a conflagration, it leaps from forest to forest.
>
> —Romain Rolland

(a) The Spinozistic Approach

'By wonder are we saved', was Plato's *ipse dixit*. This clearly indicates the nature of philosophical approach in those legendary days of Greece and Rome. They philosophized with a sense of fascination. Nature presented itself to men as a colossus and stirred them to thought.

With Descartes, philosophy started from doubt. We must approach the term of metaphysics as we do that of physics, i.e., with a questioning mind. We enter through the portals of doubt to the mystery of the dark and the unknown. As Descartes introduces himself, "Because I wished to give myself entirely to the search after truth, I thought that it was necessary for me to reject as absolutely false anything as to which I could imagine the limit round or certainty [..] And since all the same thoughts and imaginations which we have while awake may also come to us in sleep, without any of them being at the same time true, I resolved to assume that anything that ever entered into my mind was no more true than the illusions of my dreams."

The world was, for Descartes, dark and in it, man was, as it were, sailing in foreign waters. Nothing is to be believed; as one who neither believes nor disbelieves, we are to enter the world. Only distinct ideas are true ideas. Beginning with doubt, Descartes's universe is undoubtedly an alien land only fit to function by foreigners. The 'I' which is because he thinks is foreign to the world; the God of Descartes who sets the world in motion is also outside the world.

Spinoza'a approach is love and sympathy—the love for knowledge and the sympathy for understanding. The problems do involve ourselves and we must approach them with the dispassionate spirit of knowing their causes. For many, it is the fascination of Plato or the doubt of Descrates. But for Spinoza, love is the only abiding rule: "Love alone knows no limits; as it increases more and more, so also it grows more and more excellent, because it is bestowed on an object which is infinite. Hence it, and it alone, can go on increasing."[1]

Descartes's approach, we have seen, makes man a stranger in the world, an eternal doubter. And as to a man who suspects, the world remains inscrutable, except by bringing in a God down from above. His solutions are imposed upon from outside. His man comes to this world and looks for tentative execution upon which he can live his life. Again questing for truth from falsehood, that I might see the way clearly in my actions and walk with confidence in this life." But with Spinoza, both man and this world are for eternity. To quote Pollock, 'It is not enough for him to satisfy the practical need of walking with confidence in this life. He is impelled by the futility of earthly desires and sets forth on the quest of man's true and perfect good.'

The *De Intellectus Emendatione*, Spinoza's spiritual autobiography stands, according to Pollock, 'as a prelude to his matured philosophy'. In it Spinoza writes, "After experience has shown me that all those things which frequently happen in social life are vain and futile; when I saw that all the objects of my fears contained nothing in themselves good or evil, but only in so far as the

1. Short Treatise II: Ch 14.

mind was moved by them, I determined at last to enquire whether there was anything which was truly good and which could be communicated, and by which alone, everything else being set aside, the mind might be affected; in find whether there was anything, which found, I might have constant and supreme joy for ever." He gives this book a sub-title, 'How the intellect may best be guided to a true knowledge of things.'

And this true knowledge is a means to true actions. Spinoza's philosophy is a testament on action; his interest is primarily ethical than metaphysical. In order to be free from error and to work for eternal joy, we should know the essence of things as it is and a way of understanding things as complete as possible. Thus his metaphysics and epistemology come after his ethics. It is no accident that his *magnum opus* goes by the same name. The point will be clearer by giving here the explanation of White in the preface to his translation of *The Ethic*. "The truth is that, this book is really an ethic. It is not primarily a metaphysic. All there is in it which is metaphysical is intended as some basis for the ethical. There have been times in the history of the world when men have thought that the science of sciences was the knowledge of self-control, of our duty to ourselves and our neighbours. Socrates, Marcus Aurelius, Antorius and Epictetus so thought and Spinoza so thought."

"Now all those things which the multitude pursue, not only provide no remedy for the maintenance of our being, but actually hinder it," thus stating the futility of the common objects of human desire, which are wealth, power and sensual pleasures. In *De Intellectus Emendatione* Spinoza's statement has a splendour that is only Socratic. He is writing for a public which has close affinity with those boisterous young 'men of Athens, who cared so much about laying up the greatest amount of money and honour and reputation and so little about wisdom and truth and the greatest improvement of the soul.'

But this world, however false and futile it may be, is not to be shunned or connived at. Man is to grow in reason and bring joy to his life. And what is more, he can achieve it and does possess the power to achieve it. This assertion of Spinoza strikes the most optimistic nerve in his philosophy. "Those who deny that men can ever attain virtue or truth, by that very denial, prevent themselves from attaining it."[2] Spinoza never fights shy of the problems of life. The more he is recoiled by their apparent scare, the more he reasons towards it. The panacea for wrong understanding is still more understanding. Giving a similar note from Amiel, 'How to free oneself from lust? The best means still is love, great love.'[3]

In IV 36 Schol. of 'Ethic', Spinoza says, "It pertains to the essence of the human mind to have an adequate knowledge of an eternal and infinite essence of God." In a letter from Voorburg, he wrote, "These disorders do not move me to laughter, nor even to tears, but rather to philosophizing, and to the better observation of human nature. I do not think it right for me to laugh at Nature, much less to weep over it, when I consider that men, like the rest, are only a part of Nature, and that I do not know how each part of Nature is connected with the whole of it, and how with the other parts. And I find that it is from the mere want of this kind of knowledge that certain things in Nature were formerly wont to appear to me vain, disorderly and absurd, because I perceive them only in part and mutilated, and they do not agree with our philosophic mind. But now I let every man live according to his own ideas. Let those, who will, by all means die for their good so long as I am allowed to live for the truth."[4]

Recapitulating, it was Spinoza's object to discover and attain some thing which would enable him to enjoy supreme, continuous and permanent happiness. His philosophy aims at "tranquilizing the mind of the individual and elevating social life."[5] Thus he writes in another place, "I have carefully abstained from deriding human actions, from pitying them or hating them; I merely desired to understand them. Faced by passions such as love, hatred, anger, envy, variety, pity and other movements of the soul, I have tried to look upon them not as vices, but as properties characteristic of human nature; just as warmth and cold, tempests, thunder and other phenomena are characteristic of the atmosphere, being necessary

2. Short Treatise II. 8.
3. Amiel: Phillne: p. 28.
4. Letter no. 30.
5. Ethic II. 49 Schol.

albeit inconvenient, and being produced by given causes in terms of which we try to understand them."[6]

Thus, Spinoza's is the finding of the individual in the whole, and the particular in the general. His man is a man in society, his mind bears the essence of the eternal mind and his *natura naturata* is begotten from the *natura naturans*. This approach of relative evaluation, he follows only by the sanction of reason. The fragmentary experience of the world of particulars has no place in his scale of values. To the empiricist, he asks, "How can we possibly be sure that his experience of a few particulars can serve him as rule for all?"[7]

Joy, to Spinoza, consists in knowing the truth. It follows unconditionally from the axioms that he establishes at the outset. Spinoza's intellectual honesty is conspicuous everywhere. 'He fearlessly draws out the consequences of his first principles, nowhere consciously camouflaging their import despite the fact that they are often issued in conflict not only with religious dogma, but even with the obvious appearance of everyday experience. Spinoza was never afraid of persecution, nor even of appearing absurd (as judged by common sense)'. Truth is always naked, it shines with no colour, it needs no label to justify itself. As Spinoza says, "Truth is its own standard. Just as light reveals both itself and darkness, so truth is the standard of itself and of the false."[8] How near it comes to 'Vedanta' which holds truth to be self-shining!

Thus giving truth the first preference, Spinoza also gives science and superstition their due place. Science becomes free to unveil the mysteries of the universe. Theology, with its age-long appendage to magic and miracle is curbed down. To a correspondent, who seeing the imperfections of man, pleads for a place for them, Spinoza replies, "I recognize with you the weakness of man. But on the other hand, let me ask you whether we petty men have so great a knowledge of Nature that we can determine how far its force and power extends and what is beyond its power? Since no one can presume this without arrogance, therefore, one may, without boasting, explain miracles by

---

6. Tr. Pol. I-4.
7. Sot Treatise: II Ch. I.
8. Ethic II 43 Schol.

natural causes as far as possible, and as to those which we can neither explain nor prove, because they are absurd, it will be better to suspend judgement about them, and, as I said, to base Religion solely on the wisdom of its teaching."[9]

The *naivete* of Spinoza is unique. A lover of truth at the cost of everything else he had ever been, he does not even care if the individual man is reduced to a mode in his all-embracing Nature, to one of its innumerable modes. Only he, who can steer his reason clear through the passions and prejudices, can get access to the temple of the right knowledge. "Away with this deadly superstition, acknowledge the reason which God has given you, and cultivate it, if you would not be numbered among the brutes"—thus he boldly affirms, in a letter to Burgh.[10] His approach, then, is that of a child, simple, straight and unsophisticated. Thomas Huxely uplisted the same spirit when he wrote, "Sit down before a fact as a little child, be prepared to give up every pre-conceived notion, follow humbly wherever and to whatever abysses nature leads." The above can be paralleled by the following saying of Jesus, "Let the children come to me, do not try to stop them, for the kingdom of God belongs to such as they. I tell you, whoever does not accept the kingdom of God as a child shall not enter it at all."[11]

(b) The Method Geometrico

Spinoza followed the geometric method. Geometry is supposed to be the most abstract of all the branches of mathematics, which is, again, the most abstract of all the departments of knowledge. In geometry, demonstration starts with some axioms or first principles and from the nature of the axioms, the conclusions follow. The truth of the axioms is intuitively ascertained and hence that of the conclusions which follow them.

Spinoza applies this method of geometry in his most important book, *The Ethic*. In this book, he deals with all that he has to say regarding metaphysics, logic and ethics, but gives the treatise a

---

9. Letter no. 75.
10. Letter no. 76.
11. Quoted in K.F. Mather's 'Science in Search of God'.

geometric frame. In each of the chapters, he begins with a few axioms and definitions, then proves what he has to establish, in a series of propositions, adding to each of them, scholiums or corollaries, if necessary. Thus, *The Ethic* consists of twenty-seven definitions, twenty axioms and eight postulates.

This adoption of geometric method by Spinoza does nothing but shows the philosophical tempo of the age to which he belonged. The 17th century in Europe was a period of scientific investigations. The new spirit had already replaced the old, and the man of superstition was turning over a new leaf as a man of science. Though Descartes is called the father of modern philosophy, the birth of the new spirit can be traced still to earlier an time, to that of Bacon. Bacon's *Navum Organon* engendered a new approach to knowledge. The scientific current, of course, had already set in. With Copernicus, Galileo and Kepler, the world had much advanced in the field of physical experiments. The physicist, William Gilbert had proclaimed the 'new style of philosophizing' as opposed to the 'old dreaming of things that are not.' Bacon challenged the validity of the Greek syllogistic reasoning and set forth new models. The right approach to truth, according to Bacon, presupposed a thorough expurgation of the mind. 'It must cleanse itself of its prejudices—the false images or idols, that have misled it.' To all sorts of deceptive notion Bacon gave the name 'Idol" 'Everyone has a cave or den of his own, which refracts and discolors the light of nature.'

This spirit outlived Bacon through the centuries and was adopted by all who came after him. Though taking the new spirit of enquiry, many of the philosophers abandoned Bacon's method. The latter's method was inductive, to study facts, classify them and integrate them to a principle of truth was his method. But thinkers like Hobbes, Descartes and Spinoza saw a new possibility in the deductive method. These men, to quote Henry Thomas, 'abandoned the flicker of the candle to plunge into the darkness beyond; and having made their plunge, they found their way illuminated by the stars. These men worked from hypotheses to facts, rather than from facts to laws.'[12]

Logic was now applied to speculative thought. With Hobbes, it advanced another step. If we go on giving our individual interpretation

12. Living World of Philosophy, p. 85.

to words, our ideas will be at war with one another. Hence, to avoid clash, we ought to be objective and impersonal as far as practicable. 'Logic must become a demonstration of absolute principles rather than an expression of relative prejudices.' Then, as Thomas writes in the above book, 'the best medium for logic—the test of all sciences—is geometry. For here we have both formulae and facts that are true for all time, to all men, regardless of shifting impermanence of the world.' Descartes, who based his philosophy on doubt, also hinted at the possibility that the geometrical method can also be applied in proving metaphysical truths. Man is considered by him as a part of nature. And therefore he is subject to the laws of nature as other things are.

Spinoza's novelty was in applying, in actual practice, this new method, as anticipated by Descartes. To him also, geometry was the 'shortest distance between the mind of man and the center of truth.' In the appendix to the first part of *The Ethic*, he wrote, "The truth might forever have remained hid from the human race, if mathematics, which looks not to the final cause of figures, but to their essential nature and the properties involved in it, had not set another type of knowledge before them."

It is worthwhile, to render in full, the more comprehensive explanation of the geometric method given by Edward Caird. "Confusion of thought arises from the fact that we put ourselves, our desires and feelings and interests, into our view of things; that we do not regard them as they are in themselves in their essential nature but look for some final cause, that is, for some relation to ourselves by which they may be explained. But to understand things is to see how all that is true of them flows from the clear and distinct idea expressed in their definition, and ultimately it is to see how all truth flows from the essential *Dei*, just as geometrical truth flows from the idea of space. To take a mathematical view of the universe, therefore, is to raise ourselves above all consideration of the end or tendency of things, above the fears and hopes of morality, into the region of truth and necessity. [..] And Spinoza only wishes that the same universality and freedom of thought, which belongs to mathematics, because its objects do not interest the passions, should be extended to those which do interest them."[13]

---

13. Essays on Literature & Philosophy, Vol. II., p. 335.

The application of geometric method by Spinoza has been the victim of much criticism. Many see in this a weak point in Spinoza. According to Pollock, Spinoza's adoption of the geometric method 'gives to his work a needless air of abstruseness and technicality.' For the same reason, Windelband, rather in a jesting temper, calls the Spinozistic system, a mathematical pantheism. According to Hoffding, "Spinoza failed, owing to this method, to give his own ideas their true force. Their content is not adopted to this mode of treatment and his proofs are therefore frequently untenable. Nor does the method pursued in his treatment correspond with the method by which he discovered his theory."[14]

The criticism is the harshest in Melamed's *Spinoza and Buddha.* Apart from the fact that geometry is not a happy method of philosophy, Melamed points out that Spinoza has failed to apply it thoroughly and hence the *Ethic* suffers from many inner contradictions. Baumann has shown the artificiality and untenability of Spinoza's axioms. Not only the demonstrations, but also the very axioms are often questionable. Keyser, the author of 'Mathematical Philosophy' and an admirer of Spinoza also admits that the latter's method is one 'grand failure' but perorates saying that illustrious failures fall to the lot of none but illustrious men.' As Melamed justifies his position, mathematics is concerned with externalities, religion with inner processes. The former looks at life from the façade, seers and artists look beyond the façade. Spinoza, by applying mathematics to philosophy, showed his eagerness to attain apodictic truth. His mathematical procedure was dubious. In his *Ethic*, which, he says, is 'ethica ordine geometrico demonstrata', he violates the very laws of geometry. Often he argues in a circle and heaps up tautology upon tautology. A demonstration, which adds nothing to the proposition or to the definition, is not geometry but tautology. His illogical treatment of philosophy of 'more geometrico' condemns creative philosophy to 'sterility.'

The question now arises, whether Spinoza's adoption of geometric method was a part of the Spinozistic way of reasoning or was it a mere reflection of the scientific age he was in. Mathematics and scientific spirit in general had caught hold of the people of the

---

14. Brief History of Modern Philosophy, p. 57.

age and it may not have been unnatural for Spinoza to have given this model to the structure of his philosophy. But Weber and Perry hold the former view. They say, "This method of exposition is not an arbitrary form or a provisional framework, it is a piece of the system and constitutes its permanent skeleton. When Spinoza treats of the world, of man and his passions, it is because in principle and in fact he sets as great a value upon these objects of philosophy as the geometer upon his. [..] It is not his method that leads him to mathematical determinism, on the contrary he employs it because, from the very outset, he views the world from the geometrical, ie. deterministic standpoint."[15] As the geometrician deals with his planes and figures as amoral and without any end, so they say, Spinoza also does not attribute any purpose to Nature.

Whatever may be the truth, this much is clear that Spinoza got the idea of this new method from Descartes. The method attracted him for its freedom from all bias. Nor was this geometrical method adopted by Spinoza only. As Windelband records in his *History of Philosophy*,[16] this was also followed after Spinoza in Germany by Jung and Weigel. In the 18th century, Wolff pursued this line in his Latin text books. And Puffendorf deduced the entire system of Natural right by this method. Leibnitz also followed this method in writing a political brochure and had opined that "Philosophical controversies would find their end for the first time when philosophy would once make its appearance in us as clear and certain a form as that of a mathematical calculation."

'Mathematical Rationalism' is the name given by Paulsen to Spinoza's new method. The very recent symbolic school of logic espoused by Betrand Russell and others, strives to develop a 'new' logic of mathematics to serve as an anchorage in the shifting currents of modern science. Russell declares that every human decision 'can be affected by mathematical rules.' He further writes, "Mathematics, rightly viewed, possesses not only truth but supreme beauty—a beauty cold and austere like that of sculpture [..] yet sublimely pure, and capable of a stern perfection such as only the greatest art can show."[17]

---

15. History of Philosophy, p. 259.
16. Windelband's, p. 397.
17. Philosophical Essays, p. 73.

After testing both the sides of applying a cold geometrical method to the living realm of ideas, what might have been Spinoza's intention can be fairly surmised. The title of his book signifies that it has been demonstrated in the order of geometry. Only as far as the order of demonstration is concerned, not a whit more than that. Spinoza's life was the practical book where his philosophical conclusions were worked out daily by a strenuous and routined life of activities. Similarly, Spinoza might have wished that the structure of his book would reflect the same puritan austerity as did its content, even at the risk of making it outwardly dry. This argument is supported by Caird when he writes, "What recommends the geometrical method to Spinoza is, not only its apparent exactness and necessity of its sequence, but its disinterestedness."[18] And also by Ratner when he says, "Spinoza did not choose the geometrical method because he thought his philosophy too profound for ordinary exposition; nor did he choose it because he was enmeshed in medieval philosophic calculation. He chose it because his fundamental aim was to establish ethics on a thoroughly tested scientific foundation."[19]

Whatever might have been Spinoza's intention, it must not be overlooked that it is only the order of demonstration that the 'method geometrico' is applied to. Because of this novel experiment, the structure may have lost its shine, but in no way does it affect the value of the philosophy itself. We must, therefore, distinguish between the form and the content and should not, in our dislike for the method, fail to do justice to the content. "We can not understand Spinoza by jumping him," remarks White.

Let us close the chapter with a passage from Will Durant. "To our more loosely textured minds, the result is an exhausting concentration of both matter and form; and we are tempted to console ourselves by denouncing his philosophic geometry as an artificial chess-game of thought in which axioms, definitions, theorems and proofs are manipulated like kings and bishops, knights and pawns, a logical solitaire invented to solace Spinoza's loneliness. Order is against the

---

18. Essays on Literature and Philosophy, Vol. II. p. 335.
19. His Introduction in the 'Philosophy of Spinoza' (Modern Library, no. 60).

grain of our minds; we prefer to follow the straggling lines of fantasy and to weave our philosophy precariously out of our dreams. But Spinoza had but one compelling desire to reduce the intolerable chaos of the world to unity and order. He had the northern hunger for truth rather than the southern lust for beauty; the artist in him was purely an architect, building a system of thought to perfect symmetry and form.

> [..] Spinoza is not to be read, he is to be studied. You must approach him as you would approach Euclid, recognizing that in these brief two hundred pages, a man has written down his life-time's thought with stoic sculptury [..]."[20]

(c) Substance, Attributes and Modes

> —"*Know in thy self and the world one self-same soul*
> *Banish the dream that sunders the part from the whole.*"—
>
> —Shankaracharya

Spinoza entered philosophy through the theology of the scriptures and the scientific method of Descartes. In his early days, he had swallowed every bit of knowledge that existed in the sacred books of the Jews. And after studying Latin, he was engulfed by the broad daylight of reason that he detected in Descartes.

The books of the Rabbis could not satisfy him. That God was somebody above the world, and that He created it for the good of man did never convince him. If ever God is omnipotent and almighty, then, he argued in his mind, to bring Him down and adjust Him to our limitations is to deny Him the very attributes. His aversion to Jewish theology was also augmented by the bigotry and sensuality of the age. With this discontented mind, he studied Cartesianism. Only distinct ideas are true ideas; reason is the ultimate measure of values. Imagination and revolution have no place in the knowing of things. This was the thing that Spinoza was looking for and he got it in Descartes. He studied it, gave serious thoughts to it in manifold ways and at last became its interpreter and gave lessons to a learned group

---

20. Story of Philosophy, p. 186.

of young enthusiasts. By this close approach, he could see the defects in the Cartesian master and thus his original ideas struck root. With the same inquisitiveness again, with which he had entered into Descartes, he started to chalk out the outlines of his own ideas.

Descartes's world had started from 'I', which was because 'I' could think. From this first hypothesis, Descartes drew out his entire philosophical theme. From *Cogito, ergo sum*, he got the thinking mind, 'a substance whose entire nature it is to think and for whose existence there is no need of any place, nor does it depend on any material thing'. The third entity, he got, was the body. 'My body, as I can truly observe, is a substance.' Thus body, a material substance, was the passive machine, which was to be distinguished from the mind, the thinking substance and the active machine. But both the substances were undoubtedly machines and the doubter again asked the whereabouts of what he had found. There must be something, which is not a machine, not imperfect, which must be the cause of all we perceive. Whatever I can conceive very clearly and distinctly is true and this truth is more perfect than myself, which is fretted with doubts. And this was enough to posit something, which combines all the perfections of which I can have any idea, and this is God. God is perfection incarnate. 'This existence of God,' submits Descartes, 'equals and even surpasses in certitude' on the demonstrated facts of geometry'.

Thus, Descartes discovered his oasis of faith after his nightly search on the sands of doubt. He had entered it without any assumption, yet he came back with the hypothesis of God, which was no better than an assumption. This world of perception was to him a psycho-physical parallelism, a duality like the two rails running parallel to each other, and could only be interacted upon by God.

'I think, therefore I am', was easily accepted by Spinoza. But the second dictum, 'I think, therefore God is', could not convince him. He could not agree to the supposition that God is the apex upon the two points at the base, matter and mind. Then how did matter and mind interact? How could one prevail upon the working of the other? Philosophically stated, what is the *noumenon* which dominates this world of phenomenon? The world changes, our individual experiences in life are no more permanent than slips and snaps. Body perishes, reappears and again perishes. What is the reality, the essence, which outlives the appearances? This was Spinoza's problem. Perfection is not God, it is only a quality fabricated by our mind, which is imperfect. Then, how to account for the mystery of the universe?

From this Spinoza found his Substance, the eternal Substance, both in essence and existence. God is not separate from the world of matter and thought, only ruling it from His high pedestal. He is the world of both matter and thought; he is no where if not in this world. Body and mind are only his attributes, the two aspects by which he is manifested to perception. And all the individual things, including men, are the infinite number of modes that also follow from the same nature of substance.

Thus, we get the three categories of Spinoza's philosophy of existence; the Substance, the Attributes and Modes. Kettner arranges them in a diagram of a triangle, with substance as its vertex and attributes and the modes at the extremities of the base. They can also be figuratively called the Trinity or Triad of Spinoza. But in any case, they must not be misunderstood as having differing ranges of preference, the one being superior to the other two. They are one, a unity. For popular convenience, of course, we can classify Substance to the two categories of body and mind, which are only two of its many aspects.

The first part of *Ethic* establishes this trinity. The accuracy and measurement are inimitable. No where is Spinoza unnecessarily talkative nor unintelligibly laconic. The very language shows a Euclidian faith of the author in the truths he is delivering. The only problem in giving him an interesting reading is that the propositions are not arranged in the way that the categories could be established one after another. They are intermixed with and allied to one another. It will be better if we rearrange the enunciations and thus state, one by one, what Spinoza has stated about Substance, Attributes and the Modes.

Substance, God or Nature: "By Substance, I understand that which is in itself and is conceived through itself; in other words, that the conception of which does not need the conception of another thing from which it must be formed." (Def. III). "By God, I understand Being absolutely infinite, that is to say, substance consisting of infinite attributes, each one of which express eternal and infinite essence, necessarily exists." (Prop. XI) "Besides God, no substance can be nor can be conceived." (Prop. XIV) In the second corollary he writes, "It follows that the thing extended (*rem extensam*) and the thing thinking (*rem cogitantem*) are either attributes of God or affections of the attributes of God." "Whatever is, is in God, and nothing can either be or be conceived without God." (Prop. XV) "Hence it follows that God is the efficient cause of all things which can fall under the infinite intellect. It follows, secondly, that God is cause through Himself, and not through that which is contingent (*per accidens*). It follows, thirdly, that God is absolutely the first cause. (Cor. 1, 2, 3 Prop. XVI) "God is the immanent, and not the transitive cause of all things." (Prop. XVIII) "God is eternal, or, in other words, all his attributes are eternal." (Prop. XIX) "The existence and the essence of God are one and the same thing" (XX) "God is not only the cause of the commencement of the existence of things, but also of their continuance in existence, or in other words, God is the *Causa essendi rerum*." (XXIV Cor.) "God is not only the efficient cause of the existence of things, but also of their essence." (XXV) "The power of God is His essence itself." Demonstrating, "the power of God, by which He Himself and all things are and act, is His essence itself." (XXXIV) And in the appendix, he sums up, "I have shown that He necessarily exists; that he is one God; that from the necessity alone of His own nature, He is and acts; that he is, and in what way he is, the free cause of all things; that all things are in Him, and so depend upon Him that without Him they can neither be nor can be conceived; and finally, that all things have been predetermined by him, not indeed from a freedom of will or from absolute good pleasure, but from His absolute nature or infinite power." He submits that all our notions of finalism in nature are due to our age-long training in traditional myth. Because we do not know the real cause of things, we have a natural fancy to install a supernatural God who does all things for the good of man. By habit, man has made God according to his own image. But the truth is that, things follow from the necessity of the most perfect nature of God. "If men understood things, they would, as mathematics prove, at least be all alike convinced, if they were not all alike attracted."

The Attributes: "By attribute, I understand that which the intellect perceives of substance, as if constituting its essence." (Def. IV). In Def. VI, Spinoza asserts that God is the substance consisting of infinite attributes. "Each attribute of a substance must be conceived through itself" (prop. X) " God is eternal, or in other words, all His attributes are eternal." (prop. XIX)

This much is clear that Spinoza means by attributes those by which substance is manifest to the intellect. They are different aspects of the same one and only Substance. Spinoza concludes that there may be infinite number of attributes meaning thereby that the one Substance can present itself to intellect through infinite ways.

Modes: "By mode, I understand the affections of substance, or that which is in another thing through which also it is conceived." (Def. V) "Every mode which exists necessarily and infinitely must necessarily follow either from the absolute nature of some attribute of God or from some attribute modified by a modification which exists necessarily and infinitely." (XXIII) "A thing which has been determined to any action was necessarily so determined by God, and that which has not been thus determined by God, can not determine itself to action." (XXVI) "In nature, there is nothing contingent, but all things are determined from the necessity of the divine nature to exist and act in a certain manner." (XXIX)

Thus it follows that the modes are individual things but exist only as determined counterparts of God. This is clear from what Spinoza says of them. He writes, 'From the supreme power of God or from His infinite nature, infinite things in infinite ways, that is to say, all things have necessarily followed, or continually follow by the same necessity, in the same way as it follows from the nature of a triangle, from eternity to eternity, that its three angles are equal to two right angles." (Eth. I 17 Schol.) Spinoza denies them the power of will. They follow from the necessity of the absolute nature of substance or God.

Between the attributes and the modes, Spinoza mentions the existence of the infinite modes as distinguished from the finite ones; He sees an infinite connection or coherence existing in the countless finite modes of Gods and calls it an infinite mode. Seen from the attribute of extension, which pervades the entire universe of space-forms, the two infinite modes are motion and rest. And for the other attribute of thought, the *intellectus infinitus* or the infinite intellect stands beside the particular functions of ideation and will. One is reminded of David of Dinant whose pantheism wrapped God with the two phenomena of his (corporeal matter) and mind and presented the world as the self-realization of the three.

Spinoza's God is the *Causa Sui*. It exists from the necessity of its own nature. Here Spinoza annihilated the popular theory of the universe given to the people by the scriptures. Spinoza never used the word creation. Because creation means a beginning from a previous stage. So God has not created the world of things. But God is the world of things. In a letter, Spinoza writes, "men are not created, but only begotten and their bodies already existed before, although in another form."[21] As Wolf adds an annotation to it in his book, Spinoza wants to emphasise the difference between creation out of nothing and the mere transformation of already existing material. For Spinoza, things did not begin to be, the universe or substance being eternal. Then the question arises, if universe or substance is eternal, then what does Spinoza mean when he says that God is the cause of all the modes, or that without God, the modes will be impossible? But when Spinoza uses 'causality,' he does not give it the same meaning as we give it ordinarily, as an antecedent to something, which follows consequently from it. "With Spinoza, it means not, 'God creates the world', but 'He is the world.' Spinozism is a consistent identification of the relation of cause and effect with that of ground and consequent. The causality of the deity is, therefore, not in time, but is eternal, that is, timeless, and true knowledge is a consideration of things *sub quadam aeternitatis specie*."[22]

It is necessary to make one thing clear, the meaning which Spinoza gives to eternity. This word has often been misunderstood by many critics who have made the ideas of Spinoza a medley of complicated arguments. By eternal, Spinoza does not mean infinite time but only timelessness. That God eternally exists means that God is without beginning. In the eighth definition of Part I, it is stated, "By eternity, I understand existence itself, so far as it is conceived necessarily to follow from the definition alone of an eternal thing." This point can also be supported by a statement made by Pringle-Pattison,—"the term 'eternal' does not mean endless continuance in time, but a quality of experience which transcends time altogether. Thus, in Spinoza, where the contrast is specially emphasized, eternal means rational necessity."[23]

---

21. Letter no. 4.
22. Windelband, *History of Philosophy*, p. 418.
23. *Idea of Immortality*, p. 136.

Many critics detect a confusion in Spinoza's treatment of attributes. The crux of the doubt is, why Spinoza, though anticipating an infinite number of attributes, deals with only two of them. If he conceives the human mind as sensing only two attributes, how does he presume that there is an infinite number of them? Apart from this, there is also another point of contention for many of his interpreters. They can not understand the way in which Spinoza connects the two attributes of matter and thought to his all-pervading Substance. In the words of Martinue, "by bringing in the attributes, Spinoza poised his philosophy in an unstable equilibrium."[24] These two attributes are often described as the Achilles heel of Spinozistic system. Tschirnhaus, in a letter to Spinoza, wrongly infers from the theory of the attributes that there must be constituted as many worlds as there are attributes of God."[25] Many others also have accused Spinoza of pluralism. K. Thomas has pointed out that the attributes are each substances for there is little to distinguish one from the other. If this is taken for granted, then Spinozism falls into pluralism and polycosmism. Melamed remarks that Spinoza's attributes are often 'puzzling' and philosophers have given variegated opinions on them. Erdmann solves the incompatibility between Substance and the attributes by reducing the latter to mere forms of conception in the human subject. 'Attributes is what our mind sets up in order to constitute a way of conceiving substance,' so that it is but a subjective device and has no place in God or Substance. Hartmann opines that the presumption of the infinite number of attributes was only a deductive whim. Kuro Fisher explained the point by saying that they are merely forces of God. God, being the 'Efficient Cause', distributes itself into all the varieties of force, that are the individual things. Lastly, Pollock's interpretation is that the attributes should be regarded as 'aspect ' of one Substance. The last explanation comes nearest to the point. But all doubts can be best answered by reverting to Spinoza himself. He writes in *Ethic*: "We can not conclude that they (attributes) constitute two beings or two different substances, for this is the nature of Substance that each of its attributes is conceived through itself, since all the attributes which Substance possesses were

24. Martinue's p. 189.
25. Letter no. 63.

always at the same time in itself, nor could one be produced by another; but each expresses the reality or being of Substance."[26] In letter no. 27, he writes, " As the patriarch that was called by the two names of Jacob and Israel, under different aspects, each of which included the whole reality of the man, so our minds apprehend the absolute, substance in two ways each of which expresses its whole nature." "They are different definitions of the same Reality, just as a curve may be defined geometrically by the mode of generating it, or algebraically by its equation."[27] Our approach to knowledge varies from man to man and so it is not illogical to suppose that one idea is often explained in many ways, yet all the explanations extending it-self, in its own way, to the entire idea. Wolf writes in his annotation to Letter No. 63, "Substance was not merely the sum of distinct attributes, but their organic unity—Substance is the interconnected system of Attributes,— interconnected just in so far as they are the forces or the expressions of the same and only Substance." And as for the other doubt that what did Spinoza mean by suggesting an infinite number of attributes, it can be said, in brief, that Spinoza did this not to close the door for other approaches as might possibly come. For the present, he went on developing his thesis on the assumption of the two attributes that had been sensed by him. This merely indicates the natural liberality Spinoza had in philosophizing, and need not move doubters to spin out recurring complications.

In the scholium to Prop. XXVIII, Spinoza explains what he means by *natura naturans* and *natura naturata*. "By *natura naturans* we are to understand Substance which express eternal and infinite essence, that is to say, God in so far as He is considered a free cause. But by *natura naturata* I understand, everything which follows from the necessity of the nature of God, or of any one of God's attributes, that is to say, all the modes of God's attributes in so far as they are considered as things which are in God and which, without God, can neither be nor can be conceived. Creative nature is the *natura naturans* and the other is the created Nature. In the Indian philosophical terminology, the former can be called *Karya*—Brahma and the latter, the— *Karana* Brahma of the one Nature or God. The

---

26. Part I, 10 Schol.
27. Letter no. 9.

terms go back, for their historical origin, to Bruno and also to Thomas Aquinas who used *natura naturans* as meaning God. Spinoza only gave the terms a new implication. In the words of Joachim, "God as free cause is *natura naturans, natura naturata* is all the modes of God's attributes. The latter is not the world of sense-perception, but the universe in all its articulation as a perfect understanding would grasp it, if that understanding apprehended it as the effect of God's causality."

Worried of Spinoza's genetic delineation of created things from the eternal essence of Nature, many critics complain that, with Spinoza, all creation is of the same kind and essence. If everything that is, follows equally from God, the sceptic points out, should we not conclude that Spinoza does not admit of different grades of existence? That this notion is wrong is ably shown by Joachim. "God as the necessary consequent of his free causality is *natura naturata*, an ordered system of modes following with coherent necessity from *natura naturans*. But though all things follow with the same inevitable necessity from God's nature, they differ from one another in degree of perfection or reality; and indeed the difference is not only of degree, but also of kind." Spinoza writes to a correspondent, "For although a mouse is as dependent on God as an angel is, and sadness as much as joy, yet a mouse can not, therefore, be a kind of angel, or sadness a kind of joy. [..] And if the question is this, whether men who slay and those who give alms, are not equally good or perfect, I again say 'No'."[28] In letter no. 19, he writes, "The criminal expresses God's will in his own way, just as the good man in his; but the criminal is not on that account comparable with the good man. The more perfection a thing has, the more it participates in the divine nature and the more it expresses God's perfection. The good have incalculably more perfection than the vicious, and therefore, their 'virtue' is not to be compared with the 'virtue' of the vicious."

To continue Joachim's, "It is in *natura naturata*, the eternal system of modes, that these degrees of perfection or reality are exhibited. For there is an order in the sequence of the modes from God's nature, and on that order, their degree of perfection depends. The order is not a temporal but a logical one. There is no before and

28. Letter no. 23.

after in the relation of the modes; to God, all modes are the eternal consequence of God's causality. But there is a logical priority and posteriority; and on this, their degrees of reality depend."[29] Spinoza can also, in this connection, be quoted thus, "That effect is the most perfect which is produced by God immediately; and the more mediating causes which any effect requires, the less perfect it is."[30]

Three things can here be recorded only in passing, as they will be explained at length in the pages that follow; the meaning Spinoza gives to will, intellect and perfection. "By the intellect we do not understand absolute though, but only a certain mode of thought." (XXXI. Demon.) In the next proposition he also affirms that will is only a certain mode of thought and cannot be called a free cause, but can only be called necessary." And towards the end of the Appendix, he gives what he understands by perfection. "The perfection of things is to be judged by their nature and power alone; nor are they more or less perfect because they delight or offend the human senses, or because they are beneficial or prejudicial to human nature." The idea of perfection should be wholly objective and must not be perverted by transferring our own ideas to them.

The last thing is about the essence and the existence of Nature. The one implies the other and both are co-existent. God is immutable and all his attributes are immutable; for if they were changed as regards their essence, which is absurd. "The existence of God and his essence are one and the same thing." (XX) In the Appendix, Spinoza makes this still clearer. "God's decrees were decreed by God himself from all eternity, for otherwise imperfection and inconstancy would be proved against Him. But since in eternity, there is no when, nor before, nor after, it follows from the perfection of God alone that He neither can decree nor could ever have decreed anything else than that which He has decreed; that is to say, God has not existed before His decrees, and can never exist without them." How this idea is echoed even in the present age, when Gandhi, the God-intoxicated modern man upholds that "He and His law are one."[31] "God himself is both the Law and the Law-giver."[32]

29. A Study of the Ethic of Spinoza, p. 73.
30. Ethic. I. App.
31. Harijan, 24.3.46.
32. Harijan, 14.4.46.

(d) The Human Mind

"I pass on now to explain those things which must necessarily follow: from the essence of God, or the Being eternal and infinite, not indeed to explain all these things—but to consider those things only which may conduct us, as it were, by the hand, to a knowledge of the human mind and its highest happiness."

Thus introducing his reader to the second part, Spinoza first gives, in clear terms, what he means by God. He warns the reader not to posit any free will or the sovereign right over all existing things in God in the same way as we do in kings and emperors. "For it is not possible for any one properly to understand the things I wish to prove unless he takes great care not to confound the power of God with the human power and rights of kings." (III Schol.) "The being of substance does not pertain to the essence of man, or in other words, substance does not constitute the form of man," thus he reiterates in the tenth proposition. His God is one, and the "idea of God (*Idea Dei*) from which infinite number of things follow in infinite ways, can be one only." (IV)

Let us now represent, in Spinoza's own words, the various theses established through the propositions in the second part. "By body, I understand a mode which expresses in a certain and determinate manner the essence of God in so far as it is considered as the thing extended." (Def. 1) "Thought is an attribute of God, or God is a thinking thing (prop. I) "Extension is an attribute of God or God is an extended form one and the same substance, which is now comprehended under this attribute and now under that. A mode of extension and the idea of that mode are one and the same thing expressed in two different ways." (VII Schol.) Thus Spinoza establishes the body-mind unity.

Then he proceeds on to the epistemological counterpart. How far can we know reality? How can we know the truth? He affirms at the outset that "the human mind is a part of the infinite intellect of God." (IX. cor) Again in XX, he writes, "There exists in God the idea or knowledge of the human mind which follows Him." So also with the human body. "Every idea of any body or actually existing individual thing necessarily involves the eternal and infinite essence of God." (XLV) The human body is composed of 'a number of individuals of diverse nature' and the idea of 'the formal being of the human mind is not simple, but is composed of a number of ideas.' "The mind is not in error because it imagines, but only in so far as it is considered as wanting in an idea which excludes the existence of those things which it imagines as present." (XVII. Sch.) "The mind has no adequate knowledge, as often as it perceives things in the common order of nature, that is to say, as often as it is determined to the contemplation of this or that externally—namely, by a chance coincidence, and not as often as it is determined internally; for whenever it is internally disposed, it then contemplates things clearly and distinctly." (XXIX. Sch.).

"All ideas, in so far as they are related to God, are true." (XXXII) "Every idea which in us is absolute, that is to say, adequate and perfect, is true. (XXXIX)" Falsity consists in the privation of knowledge, which inadequate, that is to say, mutilated and confused ideas involve." (XXXV)

Our knowledge, Spinoza divides into three classes. In the first, he includes knowledge from vague experience and signs, better called by him knowledge from opinion or imagination. Reason constitutes the second kind of knowledge. The third kind is that intuitive science that advances from an adequate idea of the formal essence of certain attributes of God to the adequate knowledge of the essence of things. "Knowledge of the first kind alone is the cause of falsity; knowledge of the second and third orders is necessarily true." (XLI). He who has a true idea, knows at the same time that he has a true idea, nor can he doubt the truth of a thing." (XLIII) "The knowledge of the eternal and infinite essence of God which each idea involves is adequate and perfect." (XLVI). "The human mind possesses an adequate knowledge of the eternal and infinite essence of God." (XLVII) And in the scholium, Spinoza adds, "The reason why we do not possess a knowledge of God as distinct as that which we have of common notions, is that we can not imagine God as we can bodies; and because we have attached the name of God to the images of things which we are in the habit of seeing, an error we can hardly avoid, in as much as we are continually affected by external bodies."

Then Spinoza comes to the problem of free-will, "It is not of the nature of reason to consider things as contingent but as necessary." (XLIV) Hence, it follows that it is through the imagination alone that we look upon things as contingent both with reference to the past and the future. "Men are deceived because they think themselves free, and the sole reason for thinking so is that they are conscious of their own actions and ignorant of the causes by which those actions are determined." (XXV sch.) "In the mind there is no absolute or free will, but the mind is determined to this or that volition by a cause, which is also determined by another cause, and this again by another, and so on *ad infinitum*." (XLVIII). "In the mind there exists no absolute faculty of willing or not willing. Only individual volitions exist, that is to say, this and that affirmation and this and that negation."

In the sixth definition, Spinoza declares that by reality and perfection, he means the same thing. What is real is also perfect. The world of reality is the perfect world. This assertion can be well read in relation to a proposition in the first part, which says that "things could have been produced by God in no other manner nor in any other order than that in which they have been produced." To believe that God could have made better things than have been created is to make him imperfect. Everything has been represented in its best and most perfect way. It is only by our cabined understanding of things that we imagine them as imperfect and seek perfection in some Utopian standard of things. But in the eyes of God, who is clear and harmonious, understanding the existing things are never crippled and confined. In the divine order of existence, there is no distinction between the real and confined. In the divine order of existence, there is no distinction between the real and the perfect; between the real and the ideal. Let us see the problem as elucidated in the following passages. "But what is perfection? It is that state in which all the conditions of existence are present. And what are these conditions? On what is the existence of an object based? It is based on the harmonious concord of its parts. For all things are compound, consisting of single parts through whose cooperation alone the living whole is formed. [..] Now the more perfectly the single parts harmonize together, the more will the whole be capable of existence, the more will it have reality."[33] Again, "The ideal is not something unnatural, something artificially constructed; on the contrary, it is nature in its in most being [..] reality and perfection in a thing are identical, seeing that the more perfectly it is in all its parts, the more

33. Hermann Triick, *The Man of Genius*, p. 22.

capacity for existence, the more vital truth and the more reality it will possess."[34]

Another new theory of Spinoza was regarding motion and rest. He says in the first axiom that all bodies are either in a state of motion or rest. This theory was marked with a great advance in the field of dynamics and also in other departments of physics. The Greek philosophers had often wondered about the flash of movement all around and hence their God was attributed to be the 'Prime Mover'. The same blocked notion was in vogue till Descartes. He proclaimed that mind and body were two disconnected phenomena. But how had they started to move in the beginning? Whence the motion? And Descartes brought in the same theological solution, an alloy of his doubt and helplessness that the world had been set to motion by God. But with Spinoza, dynamics turned over a new leaf and was rescued from all theological trammels. Motion and rest are in the things, in fact they are their very properties. The investigator's ken was, for the first time in the history of science, cleared of all extra-mundane stumbling blocks. So also was metaphysics. Both the scientist and the metaphysician, till then bound by saucy doubts and fears, hailed the new truth that motion is not 'put into' immobile matter, but that matter 'is' motion and rest.

"The will and the intellect are one and the same thing', thus Spinoza identifies the two. (49 cor.) This assertion is quite irritating to critics who are too prejudiced to welcome any idea that is foreign to them. It is important to take note of the meaning that Spinoza gives to the word 'will.' His 'will' is not the same as the word means in common usage. Philosophically viewed, he means by will, "a faculty of affirming or denying, but not a desire, a faculty by which the mind affirms or denies that which is true or false and not a desire by which the mind seeks a thing and turns away from it." (48 Sch) And next he improves upon, "In the mind, there is no volition or affirmation and negation excepting that which the idea, in so far as it is an idea, involves." (49) The will and the intellect are nothing but the individual volitions and ideas themselves.

"Substance thinking and substance extended are one and the same substance, which is now comprehended under this attribute and

---

34. *Ibid*, p. 24.

now under that." This is often called the 'Identity Hypothesis.' But from this, it should not be mistaken that body and mind are one and the same thing. The two never interact upon each other. Spinoza wants to establish only this much that the mental and the corporeal should not be conceived as representing two substances, but the only Substance, that is God. Spoken in the plainest of terms, they each form an aspect of the same force that is Substance.

Before Spinoza, the theory of interaction explained the relation between body and mind. Though Descartes separated them as two parallel lines that never meet, he had to call in the 'animal spirits' to explain the mind-body communication. He had the conception known as *concursus Dei* (the co-operation of God), which assumed that God cooperating, communication between the body and the soul could be possible. Descartes's followers like Geulinx manipulated the theory of occasional causes which meant that the mind-body interaction was actuated by a special operation of God's power. This anthropomorphic notion of giving 'special powers' to God, the Dispenser, is ridiculous and rests upon a miracle. Leibnitz, the German contemporary of Spinoza had also another theory to account for the same. He fancied that mind and body are like two clocks, some how wound to run from eternity and so they have a mutual correspondence just like two clocks keeping the same time. This is technically called the Theory of Pre-established Harmony. Spinoza tried to solve the same problem not by making one influencing the other, but by accepting both of them as the two aspects of the same Reality.

To this day also, the problem has remained unresolved. So it will be too early to pass any opinion upon Spinoza. But his approach to the problem is strengthened by the fact that, he has, after him, a train of wise and worthy followers. We can quote only one of them; Julian Huxley, one of the modernists of scientific repute, writes, "In any case, I believe in the unity of mind and matter in the one ultimate world-substance, as two of its aspects. Mental and material are thus, to my belief but two aspects of one reality, two abstractions made by us from the concrete ground of experience; they can not really be separated, and it is false philosophy to try to think them apart."[35].

35. Religion without Revelation, p. 27.

Quoting Henry Thomas, "The mind of matter and the matter of mind are but the opposite engravings upon the coinage of truth."[36]

Now that we have come through the metaphysical and the logical portion of the 'Ethic', let us stop and examine what type of a theory of the Universe did Spinoza uphold. Was it pluralism or monism, monotheism or pantheism? Spinoza was ex-communicated from the Synagogue as an atheist. His first biographer, Colerus, had cursed him in the name of Satan. The Opera Posthuma was suppressed by the Dutch Government as 'profane, atheistical and blasphemous.' But in course of the centuries after his death, Spinoza has been variously interpreted by various authors. From his theory of an infinite number of attributes, it is supposed that Spinoza preached pluralism. Because he started with one God, many paint him as a monotheist. And also because he exalted matter and identified it with mind in Substance, many wise philosophers describe him as a pantheist. Which of the blocks does then Spinoza belong to?

That he was never a pluralist is clear enough. But those who read only pluralism in his philosophy misread it. Again, Spinoza cannot be assigned to be a monotheist because he never imagined any transcendent God nor personified Him. His God or substance was here upon this earth, not apart from it, or pervading it from a distance. He is, as Dr. Whitehead thinks Him to be, in the following passage: "Spinoza's one Substance is for me the one underlying activity of realization individualizing itself in an interlocked plurality of models."[37]

God is everywhere. Everything bears in it the essence of God and follows from His divine necessity. Does Spinoza then not come to the mould of pantheism? Yes, but in a restricted sense. His pantheism does not imply life in all material things, it does not preach naturism. It should be viewed as distinct from panpsychism, the pet notions of Fechner, Nacgeli and Wundt in science and of Wordsworth in poetry. For Spinoza, thought and extension were the two knowable aspects of God. But they each enjoy an equal status in expressing God's essence. Fechner and others have eliminated this line of distinction and so they posit a soul in every material object. Fechner writes, "It (the earth) is

---

36. Living World of Philosophy, p. 71.
37. Science and the Modern World, p. 99.

that complete. All of which our body is but a member, it is that permanent all of which our body is but a transitory part, it is to it what the whole tree is to a single twig, a permanent body is to a perishable small organ."[38] And with Nacgeli, "the same mental thread runs through all material phenomena. The human mind is nothing but the highest development on our earth of the mental processes which universally animate and move nature." This element of panpsychism can be traced back to the Greek hylozoist, Empedocles, who gave to all bodies the psychical functions of love and hate. The panpshychist among the moderns is Paulsen with his doctrine of the "World Soul." He writes, "He who lives in the real world himself, will not, if he is at all endowed with a little imagination, find it so difficult to conceive the world as a large animated body." But Spinoza is not a pantheist in this superficial sense that God is a spirit which is distributed in all things but in the truer sense that all things are in God and are modifications of him.

Kettner coins a new word for Spinoza's world-outlook. To contradistinguish it with pantheism, he calls it hentheism. "Spinoza was a hentheist, not a pantheist. The many who, from the pantheistic point of view, say everything is God, can never come to the *one reality* which unites all these separate things into one; such as land, water, air, men, beasts etc. They do not have the true idea of *oneness*. Their ideas are fragmentary in as much as pantheism presents to their mind's eye only fragments of the *one substance*, each as an entity in itself. According to Spinoza, each thing is but a modification of the *one substance*. But their pantheism eliminates for them, Spinoza's idea of the Attributes, the only bridge, so to speak, which can unite the *many* and the *one,* or which can lead them from the pan to the hen... Let them begin with the hen (one) and they will realize that the pan (everything) constitutes but the many-sidedness of the one totality. Therefore, unless we understand Spinoza as a hentheist, we can not truly be said to understand his principle."[39]

Our empirical world is ordinarily perceived as dual rather than plural. We are satisfied with calling things high and low, good and

---

38. Zend-Avesta, I. p. 179.
39. From his article published in Spinoza Quarterly, Tercentenary Number.

bad or big and small. But from the first man, who ever gave some serious thoughts to the problem of existence, most of the philosophers have visualized a unity in all this flux of passing phenomena and given all their labours to find out the essence underlying things. The world is one process or the one structure of the one force. Thinkers have given their various names for this force but the truth remains that most of them had sensed a unity in diversity, the one in the many. The Greek conception *Hen Kai Pan* (All is One) was but the name of the monistic picture that the Greek philosophers had held before them. "Listen not to me," writes Heraclitus, but to reason, and confess the true wisdom that all things are one." Melamed points out that all the European thinkers, except Plato and Spinoza, held a dualistic attitude towards the universe. But by a deeper study of the general run of philosophy, it will be clearly seen that most of the philosophers have strived to find a permanent unity over the evanescent play of phenomena, a never-changing law that may explain the ever-changing universe. Except the cynics and skeptics,—because the former 'denied without philosophising' and the latter 'philosophized without denying or accepting'—everywhere we can detect a search for the one which can embrace the many. This is the 'spiritual unanimity,' to steal a phrase from H. Thomas, which has been the common ground of all understanding.

Coming to the East, we find the idea of the One manifest in ancient Indian philosophy. With it, the world is alive with one God. But this God was often not the Lord of Heaven, the Welder of World's destiny and the record keeper of our flaws and falls. *Sarbabhūtā-ntarātmā* was the name it had given to God. In *Rigveda*, Varuna has been extolled as the one dominating power, as the ruler of the macrocosm and microcosm alike. The more we examine the Varuna hymns, the more we come to know that it is never Varuna's personality, but the leading cosmic idea underlying his conception. He is called the representative of *Rta* as the cosmic order. Whatever he is said to perform, he really achieves by force of *Rta*, which means the immanent dynamic order or inner balance of the cosmic manifestations themselves.

Sarbam Khalwidam Brahma, thus the Indian sage proclaimed the one to the ages. *Yah devah agnaū yah apsū yah Viswabhūbanamābhibsha, yah osadhisū yah banaspatisū tasmai dévāya namonamah*, thus he saluted only to the unity which underlies the outward variegatedness. *Yasmin dyouh prthivi chantarikshyamotam manah saha prānaischa sarbe tamaibaikam jānatha.* In him are woven the heaven, and the inter-space, and the mind also with all the senses. Know him to be the one support of all (Mundaka: II-5). *Atha yah atmā sa setūrbidhṛti-resham lokānām-asambhedāya.* Now, that which is the soul, is a bridge, it is a support for the preservation of all these worlds from destruction. (Chhandogya: 8/4/10 "Understand me as the knower of the Field in all fields," thus says the Geeta (Ch. XIII). Thus we see that the sacred books of ancient India reverberate with the idea of the One, in which all have their beings, and in Spinozistic terms, without whom, nothing can be or be conceived.

According to Melamed, "Spinoza hears one with Shankara. The latter's monism also was not oneness but non-duality. His 'sat' is the prototype of Spinoza's Substance. Like Shankara, Spinoza also starts with God." But this lining up of one philosopher with another is harmful and often smacks of the dangers of a hasty identification. No philosopher in history has exactly followed the footsteps of another; only the extent we can show, is how different philosophers have come very near to the same track or how they have made identical approaches. Spinoza's doctrine of Substance may not find an exact parallel, but still the doctrine stands as shining as ever, his is the one of many attempts at knowing the essence of things. His doctrine has been derided by many from various interests, and many also have seen in him the exact explanation. We may close the discussion with the remarks of Edward Caird in his essay on Cartesianism: "Spinoza's bold identification of spirit and matter, God and Nature, contains in it the germ of a higher idealism. [..] A true idealism must vindicate its claims by absorbing materialism into itself. It was, therefore, a true instinct of philosophy that led Spinoza to raise matter to the co-equal of spirit, and at the same time, to protest against the Cartesian conception of matter as mere inert mass, moved only by impulse from without. 'What were a God that only impelled the world from without?' says Goethe, 'It becomes Him to stir it by an inward energy, to involve nature in Himself, Himself in nature.'"[40]

40. Encyclopedia Britannica.

(e) This Human Nature

"*Happy is he who knows the causes of things.*"

—Lucretius

"It is true that very eminent men have not been wanting, to whose labour and industry we confess ourselves much indebted, who have written many excellent things about the right conduct of life, and who have given to mortals, counsel full of prudence; but no one, so far as I know, has determined the nature and strength of the affects, and what the mind is able to do towards controlling them," thus Spinoza takes his reader to the third part.

This part deals with the psychological portion of his *Ethic*. We, men upon earth, are subject to the humming and buzzing sensations outside us. It seems, as it were, the sensations come with such impelling force as compels us to respond to them. "There is no soul so vile, no heart so barbarous, that it is not susceptible to some kind of attachment," Rousseau wrote in his *Confessions*.[41] Many things we see as beautiful, we are attracted to them; many others are ugly to us, we are repelled from them. On many a rock of hope we anchor and flee away with fear from many others, fight shy of them. People judge us from our emotions and attachments. All through the ages, the man of virtue has been raised up and the man of sin has been cursed by all the thinking men, the philosophers. The latter have come with extraordinary grace, despised the sinful as unwanted outlaws in the world of morals and manners. The result has been that the poor wretch has always remained a wretch, only to weep over his weakness, which the divine displeasure has invoked upon him. The fallen man has been looked down as a delinquent whose ills no worldly healing can heal. But Spinoza's approach to the human emotions was new of its kind. He did not follow those 'who prefer to detest and scoff at human affects and actions than understand them.' As Gunn remarks, "Spinoza 'looked at the whole problem like a doctor rather than as a policeman." He came to the emotion-ridden man as a scientist, with all their appendent causes. As a surgeon takes a septic sore neither as a curse nor a sin, but only as a part of human

41. *Confessions*, p. 67.

body disfigured, so Spinoza saw in the emotions only a working of human mind, suffering from temporary distractions. With the sore operated upon, the body is healed; so also with the emotions rightly re-channeled, the mind can be made normal. Spinoza could not be at home with the thinkers and preachers "who regard the passions which trouble men, as vices into which they fall by their own fault and are wont to laugh at them, to weep over them, to carp at them and those who take greater pretensions to piety, seek to hold them up to abhorrence."[42]

Spinoza was no sermonizer, nor was he the God-sent rare saint to shepherd the fallen men to the hell of atonement and retribution. He was a man among the men, who were again a part in the order of the universe. He was intolerant to those who 'consider man in nature as a kingdom within a kingdom.' Because his conviction was that nothing happens in nature which can be attributed to any vice of it, for it is always and everywhere the same. Its power of acting, that is to say, its laws and rules, according to which all things are and are changed from form to form, are everywhere and always the same; so that there must also be one and the same method of understanding the nature of all things whatsoever, that is to say, by the universal laws of nature. Borrowing a few lines from the previous chapters of the 'Ethic', Nature is one in essence and existence: The one law operates in her and produces the myriads of things, darkness and light, fire and thunderstorm. One cannot be hailed as beautiful, nor another despised as deformed. In itself, Nature is neither perfect nor imperfect. "The affects of hatred, anger, envy, considered in themselves, follow from the same necessity and virtue of nature as other individual things; they have certain causes through which they are to be understood, and certain properties which are just as worthy of being known as the properties of any other thing, in the contemplation alone of which we delight. [..] And therefore I shall consider human actions and appetites just as if I were considering lines, planes or bodies."[43]

Thus, according to Spinoza, it is true that we are affected by sensations and respond to them in certain ways. This response to sensations, he technically calls affects. By affects, he means the

---

42. Trachatus Politicus. I.
43. Ethic, p. 105.

'affections of the body, by which the power of acting of the body itself is increased, diminished, helped or hindered, together with the ideas of these affections.' These affects act differently upon us as the nature of our nature may be. "I say that we act when anything is done, either within us or without us, which by that nature alone can be clearly and distinctly understood. On the other hand, I say that we suffer when anything is done within us, or when anything follows from our nature, of which we are not the cause excepting partially." (Def. II) And by an adequate cause, Spinoza means that 'whose effect can be clearly and distinctly perceived by means of the cause.' Wolf marks out a difference between the terms adequate and true in the light of Spinozistic conception. "An idea is adequate in so far as it really does enable us to unify and interconnect a certain range of observations, and if it is adequate, it is also true; because it then agrees with the observed facts. But for Spinoza, the primacy is with the adequacy of the idea because until we have the adequate idea, the facts are not yet apprehended in such a way that the idea can be said to agree with them i.e. to be true." Making easy, it follows that we act when we distinctly know the causes of things and we suffer when we are agitated by affects from outside, yet are ignorant of what they result from.

"Our mind," Spinoza goes on, "acts at times and at times suffers: in so far as it has adequate ideas, it necessarily acts; and in so far as it has inadequate ideas, it necessarily suffers." (Prop. 1) And the corollary that follows, reads: "Hence it follows that the mind is subject to passions in proportion to the number of inadequate ideas which it has, and that it acts in proportion to the number of adequate ideas which it has." Then in the third proposition, he clearly defines our action and passions: "The actions of the mind arise from adequate ideas alone, but the passions depend upon those alone which are inadequate." So the canker of all our sufferings lies not in the mind itself, nor in any of its properties. We suffer not because we have a mind; this is like thinking that we suffer from headache because we have a head. But we suffer because the mind is distracted by inadequate ideas, from its natural channel of action. This is why Spinoza says, "the passions are not related to the mind, unless in so far as it possesses something which involves negation." (3-Sch.) In the same negative way also these passions are related to individual things. The disease is not due to the nature of the body, but to the germs that come in its way, and hence they are a destructive force in relation to the body. So also our suffering does not follow from the mind; they result from the passions which obstruct the mind in its having adequate ideas.

Here, Spinoza diverts a little and establishes the mutual independence of body and mind. Neither dominates the working of the other. "The body can not determine the mind to thought, neither can the mind determine the body to motion nor rest nor to anything else, if there be anything." (2) Because our body and our mind are one and the same thing in essence, the order or concatenation of things is one, whether nature be conceived under this or under that attribute, and consequently the order of the actions and passions of our body is coincident in nature with the order of the actions and the passions of the mind. But the other assumption, as is popularly believed, that the mind moves the body to action, is a wrong one. This error is due to our being habituated to the thought that all our activities depend on the will of our mind and also to our ignorance of the powers of the body. Spinoza supports himself by arguing that 'no one as yet has understood the structure of the body so accurately as to explain all its functions.' Then he fancies that the occurrences of somnambulism are examples what the body can do even if the mind is sleeping. But in those old days of faculty psychology, the learned men were ignorant of the unconscious that has been only a very recent discovery. Thus it was easy for Spinoza to assume that body and mind were independent of each other. Weighing Spinoza's psychology against that of our time, of course, his theory is a weak one.

The notion of the superiority of the mind, he says, was a deduction from a false premise that our mind is free. He refutes the argument as he has refuted freedom in the previous chapters. "The infant believes that it is by free-will that it seeks the breast; The angry boy believes that by free will he wishes vengeance, the timid man believes that it is with free will he seeks flight; the drunkard believes that by a free command of his mind he speaks the things, which, when sober, he had left unsaid. Thus the mad man, the chatterer, the boy and others of the same kind, all believe that they speak by a free command of the mind, whilst, in truth, they have no power to restrain the impulse which they have to speak, so that experience itself, no less than reason, clearly teaches that men believe themselves to be free simply because they are conscious of their own actions, knowing nothing of the causes by which they are determined; it teaches too that the decrees of the mind are nothing but the appetites themselves, which differ, therefore, to the different temper of the body." (2. Sch.)

Now Spinoza passes on to the part that is his most excellent contribution to world philosophy, the theory of 'conatus se conservandi', or the theory of 'self-preservation.' "Each thing in so far as it is in itself, endeavours to persevere in its being." The effort by which each thing endeavours to persevere in its own being is nothing but the actual essence of the thing itself." (6&7) It should not be meant from this perseverance for self preservation that Spinoza's world is akin to the Darwinian world picture of clashes and conflicts where the species are at constant war with one another, striving to survive others in the struggle for existence. It is simply persisting in being what one is. But developing the argument in another way, to persist to be what one is, is to be according to one's own nature or essence, that is, to be in reality. And for Spinoza, reality and perfection are one and the same thing. (II Def. VI) This leads us to think that the mind in itself has a natural tendency to persist in its natural essence, that is, to free itself by getting rid of passions. But more on this later.

Pollock warns us not to misunderstand this tendency of self preservation as a mysterious power implanted in things and antecedent to their existence. This should not thus be mistaken for the Buddhistic *Karma*, the will of Schopenhauer or the unconscious of Hartmann. Because with Spinoza there is nothing like prior to existence as for him existence exists from eternity, that is, it is without beginning. Only in Herbert Spencer, Pollock finds a modern reading of Spinoza. According to Spencer, life is the continuous adjustment of internal relations to external relations. It is his struggle for existence by adjusting oneself to the changing environment. This adjustment is precisely what Spinoza means by a thing's persistence in its own being.

With this elementary principle working in all individual things, Spinoza enters into his code of the affects. The mind is conscious of its effort of self preservation: "When the effort is related to the mind alone, it is called will, but when it is related at the same time to the mind and the body, it is called appetite, which is therefore nothing but the very essence of man from the nature of which necessarily follow those things which promote his preservation and thus he is determined to those things." Also there is no difference between appetite and desire, except that desire is generally related to men in so as they are conscious of their appetites. It can, hence, be an appetite of which we are conscious. From what has been, it is plain, therefore, that we neither starve for, wish, seek nor desire anything because we think it to be good but, on the contrary, we adjudge a thing to be good because we strive for, wish, seek or desire it. (9. sch).

Here we come to the three elementary elements of joy, sorrow and desire. "Besides these three, I know of no other primary affect, the others springing from these," "Desire is the essence itself of man in so far as it is conceived as determined to any action by any one of his affections." "Joy is man's passage from a less to a greater perfection. Sorrow is man's passage from a greater to a less perfection." (The Affects: Def 1, 2, 3)

"When the mind contemplates itself and its own power of acting, it rejoices, and it rejoices in proportion to the distinctness with which it imagines itself and its power of action. When the mind imagines its own weakness, it necessarily sorrows," (53, 55) and the mind is averse to imagine those things which lessen or hinder its power and that of the body. (13. Cor)

Thus, we see that love is nothing but joy accompanied with the idea of an external cause, and hatred is nothing but sorrow with the accompanying idea of an external cause, (13. Sch.) Hatred is increased through return of hatred, but may be destroyed by love.(43) Hatred, which is altogether overcome by love, passes into love.(44)

Different men may be affected by one and the same object in different ways at different times. (51) Thus, it should be remembered, that the joy or sorrow that results from being affected, does not lie on the affect but on the nature of the man who is affected. Reducing to modern terms, the influence of emotions is the subject's nature of reacting to the perceived object. Spinoza writes, "The affect of one person differs from the corresponding affect of another as much as the essence of the one person differs from that of the other." (57) And also when the same man is affected at the same time by two contrary affects, the mental state, thus caused is the vacillation of the mind.

By good, Spinoza understands every kind of joy and everything that conduces to it; chiefly however that satisfies longing, whatever that thing may be. By evil, he means every kind of sorrow and chiefly whatever thwarts longing. But because we know the Spinozistic interpretation of good and evil, we must not misunderstand him when he states thus. There is nothing ultimately good or bad in this world. They are only qualities subjectively conferred upon things. As Taine, the French writer has remarked, vice and virtue are products just as vitriol and sugar. In introduction to his *History of English Literature* he writes, "Whether facts be moral or physical, it makes no matter. They always have their causes. There are causes for ambition, courage, veracity, just as there are for digestion, muscular movement, animal heat. Vice and virtue are products like vitriol and sugar." A thing is good or bad as we desire it or are averse to it, but not vice versa. As Shakespeare sings in *Hamlet*: "There is nothing good or bad, but thinking makes it so." Each person, therefore, according to his nature, judges or estimates what is good and what is evil, what is better and what is worse, and what is best and what is the worst (39 Sch.)

"So much for the affects which are related to man in so far as he suffers. It remains that I should say a few words about those things which are related to him in so far as he acts." So far the discourse has been on the passions, those, 'ascribed to man in so far as he is acted upon,' but there are also emotions of the active kind. In the 58th proposition, Spinoza comes to this new theme, "Besides the joys and sorrows which are passions, there are other affects of joy and sorrow which are related to us in so far as we act." He continues, "Amongst all the affects which are related to the mind in so far it acts, there are none which are not related to joy or desire." No affect of sorrow can be related to the mind in so far as it acts, but only affects of joy and desire. And the scholium adds, "All the actions which follow from the affects which are related to the mind in so far as it thinks, I ascribe to fortitude, which I divide into strength of mind and generosity." The first is the desire by which each person endeavours from the dictates of reason alone to preserve his own being. [..] The other is the desire by which the person is reasonably led to help other people and join them in friendship."

Then Spinoza sums up the chapter: "From what has been said, it is plain that we are disturbed by external causes in a number of ways, and that, like the waves of the sea agitated by contrary winds, we fluctuate in our ignorance of our future and destiny." He concludes the chapter with a categorical definition of forty-eight affects which he considers to be the most important of all.

This cold geometrical method of defining one affect after another naturally taxes much from the reader, often to the extent of losing his patience. Melamed curtly remarks that Spinoza's method of explaining the affects is reminiscent of a 'psychological primer.' This also reminds one of the enumeration of *Bhāba* in Sanskrit poetics.

But when we go deep beyond the framework, we never fail to see with what sympathy and attention Spinoza states and defines each of the affects. Spinoza's excellence lies in his masterly exposition of the passions.

Spinoza's psychology, as we have seen, is often defective when compared with that of the present century. But his new approach to the problems of mind, that of sympathetic understanding is conspicuously the modern spirit in all researches. In the early days of scientific inventions and social revolutions, the learned men looked at the world-problems as an alien fortress to be conquered. They were dreaming to conquer and subdue nature as if nature lay outside this universe. The same spirit of cruel sub-duel was current in tackling social problems also. But with the gradual dawning of the new sense upon man, the wild adventurousness gave way to sympathy, compassion and love in all the spheres of study. The new spirit has tolled the death-knell of all prejudice and narrowness. The new scientist works in the laboratory, the philosopher spends nights over the articulated world-problems, not for the pleasure of any state or sovereign, not under the obligations of any faith or fantasia, but purely from a spirit of love to know and find out new knowledge. The defective, the delinquent and the criminal have now come to be counted as men of society, and their maladies not as curses to be looked with scorn but as new fields of operation and cure. The unruly child is no longer abandoned to the mercy of the rod, the modern educationist studies him in his classes and tries to make up his defects; modern penology does not condemn the criminal as a born antisocial, it experiments upon him in the correction homes; the sexually timid youth is no longer to be done away from society, but his problem is also given serious thoughts. Thus we see that the Spinozistic spirit of accepting, without the least aversion, the problems of the work of the world just as joyously as we accept the natural shortcomings and trying to study and mend them, is the prevailing spirit of the time. In order to be able to approach the problems of the world with sympathy and sacred interest, Spinoza, in his metaphysics, brought down God to the world and sanctified all that was till then despised as flesh. With the world of existence becoming only an aspect of God's essence, all things material could shine with divine glory and become worthy of being acceded to. This unique contribution of Spinoza to the problems of the future makes him singularly the greatest personality of his age.

(f) The Man in Bondage

'*Give me that man that is not passion's slave, and I will wear him in my heart's core*' —Shakespeare

Spinoza writes in his fifteenth letter, "Let us imagine a little worm living in blood which has vision enough to discern the particles of blood, lymph etc. and reason enough to observe how one particle is repelled by another with which it comes into contact, or communicates a part of its own motion to it. Such a worm would live in the blood as we do in this part of the universe, and would regard each particle of it, not as a part, but as whole, nor could it know how all the parts are influenced by the universal nature of the blood, and are obliged to accommodate themselves to each other according to a fixed law. For if we suppose that there are no causes outside of the blood which could communicate new motions to it, and no space beyond the blood, nor any other bodies to which particles could transfer their motion, it is certain that the blood as a whole would always maintain its present state, and its particles would suffer no other variations than those which may be inferred from the given relation of the motion of blood to lymph, chyle etc. And thus the blood would require to be considered as a whole and not as a part. But since there are many other causes which influence the laws of the nature of blood, and in turn are influenced by other motions and other variations, must arise in blood which are not due to the reciprocal relation of the motion of its parts, but also to the relation between that motion and external causes. And therefore we can not consider the blood as a whole, but only as a part of a greater whole.

"Now we can think, and indeed ought to think. of all natural bodies in the same manner in which we have thought of this blood, for all bodies are surrounded by other bodies, and reciprocally determine and are determined by them to exist and operate in a fixed and definite way, so as to preserve the same ratio of motion and rest in the whole universe. Hence, it follows that everybody, in so far as it exists in a certain definite modification, ought to be considered as merely a part of the whole universe which agrees with the whole and thereby is in intimate union with all the other parts; and since the nature of the universe is not limited like that of the blood, but absolutely infinite, it is clear that by this nature with its infinite powers, the parts are modified in an infinite number of ways and compelled to pass through an infinity of variations. Moreover, when I think of the universe as a substance, I conceive of a still closer union of each part with the whole, for it is the nature of substance to be infinite, and therefore every single part belongs to the nature of the corporeal substance, so that apart from that, it neither can exist nor be conceived. And as to the human mind, I think of it also as a part of nature; for I think of nature as having in it an infinite power of thinking, which, as infinite, contains in itself the idea of all nature, and those thoughts run parallel with all existence."

This rather long passage has been adopted here to give, in Spinoza's clear words, his vision of the universe. It is a vast structure, whose actual working is beyond the ken of human knowledge. The inductive and analogical process of drawing conclusions about the nature of the universe is, therefore, wrong, and absurd. All the attributes by which we try to define nature are relative and insufficient in themselves. Nature is vast and inexhaustible, its frame is what it is. It baffles all human notions of economy because economy presupposes scarcity and there is never any scarcity in nature's means and materials. "Because to Him, material was not wanting for the creation of everything [..] the laws of this nature were so ample that they sufficed for the production of everything which can be conceived by an infinite intellect."[44]

The range of human life is small and limited and so naturally man has his preference for better and more perfect things. By a long acquaintance with earthly things he has built, in his mind, a perfect specimen of everything. And this genus-making habit he also has

44. Ethic. I. App.

extended beyond his own universe of particular knowledge, to one of whose workmanship he knows not anything. 'Men are in the habit of forming, both of natural and of artificial objects universal ideas which they regard as types of things, and which, they think nature has in view, setting them before herself as types too, it being the common opinion that she does nothing except for the sake of some end. [..] Thus we see the custom of applying the words perfect and imperfect to natural objects has arisen rather from prejudice than from the true knowledge of them." Nature never acts from any end. No deformity can be attributed to her. So, "perfection and imperfection are really only modes of thought, that is to say, notions which we are in the habit of forming from the comparison with one another of individuals of the same species or genus."

Likewise our notions of good and evil are also relative. There is nothing good and evil in itself as in nature, nothing works from any purpose. "For one and the same thing may at the same time be both good and evil or indifferent. Music, for example, is good to a melancholy person, bad to one mourning, while to a deaf man it is neither good nor bad." So by good is meant everything which, we are certain, is a means by which we may approach nearer and nearer to the model of human nature we set before us. Evil means everything, which, we are certain, hinders us from reaching that model. Or in Spinozistic definitions, "good is that we certainly know is useful to us and evil is that hinders us possessing anything that is good." (Def. 1, 2)

Spinoza deduces his man from Nature, and not vice versa. Man is a mode in the system of infinite existence. He is already a part of nature. So Spinoza deduces, "We suffer in so far as we are a part of Nature, which part can not be conceived by itself nor without the other parts." (Prop. 2) We, as men, are powerless to seek our own good defying Nature's workmanship. "The force by which man preserves in existence is limited and infinitely surpassed by the power of external causes," (3) and "It is impossible that a man should not be a part of Nature, and that he should suffer no changes but those which can be understood through his own nature alone, and of which he is the adequate cause." (4) "Hence it follows that a man is necessarily always subject to passions, and that he follows and obeys the common order of nature, accommodating himself to it as far as the nature of things requires." (4 Cor.) Man is already in bondage; he is not so strong as to live only by adequate ideas because there is the much vaster universe, which is not for man, but because it is. The external powers are so powerful that they can often supersede man's limited power to persevere in his own being.

It follows thus, 'Is not Spinoza's man reduced to a tiny and helpless germ, an insignificant mode susceptible to all the external freaks of nature?' Wherein, then, is the independence of man? We must stop here for a while and take care lest we should misunderstand what Spinoza says afterwards. Metaphysically considered, man is a part of Nature. But when we consider man as already in the world, he is there free to follow the ethical code of virtues, as is conducive to his existence. That man is such a speck of dust in the entire order or existence, does not stand against his living here upon this earth. Once in this earth, he must live here with the best of his abilities, be the earth a meagre part of the universe or determined to every action of a God who has no end before Him. Our life on this globe can never be explained away on the plea that the universal order is inexplicable. This suggests Kant, who, though in his first *Critique* concluded with man's helplessness to know the reality of things, nevertheless drew out his second *Critique*, the one of Practical Reason, wherein he outlined a complete code of conduct. Thus Kant, the rationalist announced his great work as 'destroying reason to make room for faith', and dubbed the process of reason, 'a dialectic of illusion'. Thoreau writes, "I came to this world not chiefly to make this a good place to live in, but to live in it, be it good or bad."[45]

Spinoza's metaphysics does not conclude with an uncertainty of fate. His world is not the unconnected whim-product of a capricious God. The truth is that he accepts the actual world seeing that the entire order is too big for human understanding. To take nature as what it is, is but to accept the order. And because man is too small a species and has only limited powers, he gives his moral code to be followed so that man can, with the best of his resources, accommodate himself with the world. Coming down to earth, his ethical code becomes imperative and he also elicits qualities that are certainly or in themselves good or bad.(As in prop. 27) In a letter he writes, "This inevitable necessity (of all things in nature) does not do

45. *Selections from Thoreau*, Edited by H.S. Salt, p. 251.

away with divine or human laws. For moral precepts whether they do or do not receive the form of law from God Himself, are nevertheless divine and salutary; and whether we receive the good, which follows from virtue and the love of God, from God as a judge, or whether it proceeds from the necessity of the Divine nature, it will not, on that account, be either more or less desirable, just as, on the other hand, the evils which follow on wicked actions and feelings, will not be less to be feared because they follow from them necessarily. Lastly, whether we do what we do, necessarily or contingently, we are nevertheless led by hope and fear."[46] In Spinoza's psychology, good and bad are relative terms, but coming to 'Practical Reason' or Ethic, he also senses the objective good and bad, that is, good and bad in themselves. Does this, then, out-Spinoza Spinoza? Spinoza makes himself clear in the following letter, "It is true, that in the world we act on conjecture. In ordinary life, we must follow that is most probable, but in philosophical speculations, the truth. Man would perish of thirst and hunger if he would not eat or drink until he had obtained a perfect proof that food and drink would do him good. But in contemplation, this has no place. On the contrary, we must be cautious, not to admit as true something which is merely probable. For when we admit one falsity, countless others follow."[47] Spinoza very clearly marks the distinction between metaphysical truth and truth in daily life. In the former he gives out a feeling that is almost Cartesian, but in *Ethics*, it is only the human life that concerns him. Man's good, his preservation is the highest good here. Ethics should not be confusedly lined up with metaphysics. Borrowing from Wolf's annotation to the above letter, Spinoza could agree with Bishop Butler, that 'probability is the guide of life' so far as the practical contingencies of life are concerned. But in the case of theoretical and scientific problems, his attitude is what has been expressed by Huxley, who insisted on a 'skeptical scrutiny' of the credentials of every suggestion or belief.

Spinoza's metaphysics was secondary to his ethics. He is primarily an ethical teacher than a seeker after the abstruse reality. He did not wait to know the actual truth about man. Seeing man

---

46. Letter no. 75.
47. Letter no. 56.

overwhelmed by passions, he sought to find out the ethical sanctions by which man could be free. Thus he comes very near to Gautama Buddha who also was primarily concerned with the sorrows of the world. In 'Cula-Malūkya-Ovāda' of 'Majjhima Nikāya', Buddha says to Malūkya, "If a man were struck by a poisoned arrow, and his friends and relatives called—in a skillful physician, what if the wounded man said, 'I shall not allow my wound to be treated until I know who the man is by whom I have been wounded, whether he is a noble, a *brāhmana*, a *vaishya* or *shūdra*,'—or if he said, 'I shall not allow my wound to be treated, until I know what they call the man who has wounded me, and of what family he is, whether he is tall, or small, or of middle stature; and how his weapon was made, with which he has struck me.' What would the end of the case be? The man would die of his wound... Therefore, Mālukyapūtta, whatsoever has not been revealed by me, let that remain unrevealed, and what has been revealed, let it be revealed."[48]

Thus coming down to the ethical plane, as distinguished by Spinoza from the metaphysical, we see that man is affected by passions over which he has little control. 'The force and increase of any passion and its perseverance in existence are not limited by the power by which we endeavour to persevere in existence, but the power of an external cause compared with our own power." (5 Sch.) No particular thing is found in nature which is not exceeded in power and strength by some other: but whatsoever thing be taken, another more powerful can be found whereby the first may be destroyed. Man is but a part of nature, his powers are limited and subject to be overmastered by external causes. On external causes, too, depends the strength of human passions, for passion is the modification of the mind under an external cause. Hence comes a proposition of the first practical importance, that "an affect neither be restrained nor removed unless by an opposed and stronger affect." (7) Man is a child with affectations. He is such constituted that to him, an affect due to a present existing cause, is stronger than that which proceeds from contemplation of something distant in time and space. This is why he is so weak to obey the dictates of reason alone, this is why he errs even when he knows what is good and what is bad. Is it then a folly to

48. Taken from Buḍdha by Oldenberg, p. 275.

be wise? Does increasing knowledge mean also increasing sorrow? Spinoza explains, "I say these things not because to conclude that the wise man in governing his passions is nothing better than the fool, but I say them because it is necessary for us to know both the strength and the weakness of our nature, so that we may determine what reason can do and what it can not do in governing our affects." (17 Sch.)

So much about the human weakness in its relation to the affects. Then Spinoza goes on to demonstrate what it is which reason prescribes to us, which of the affects agree with the rules of human reason and which of them are opposed to these rules.

"According to the laws of his own nature, each person necessarily desires that which he considers to be good, and avoids that which he considers to be evil. The more each person strives and is able to seek his own profit, that is, to preserve his being, he possesses the more virtue; and on the other hand, as far as he neglects his own profit, that is, neglects to preserve his own being, to that extent he is impotent. No one can desire to be happy, to act well and live well, who does not at the same time desire to be, to act and to live, that is to say, actually to exist. Living must come before living well; the desire for a virtuous life is nothing without the desire for life itself. No virtue can be considered prior to the virtue of self-preservation. The actions of a man who has inadequate ideas cannot be called virtue but a virtuous man is he who acts because he understands. When a man acts in conformity with virtue, he does nothing but acts, lives and perseveres in his being as reason dictates, from the ground of seeking his own profit. No one seeks to preserve his own being for the sake of another object." (19-25 Sch.)

All efforts which we make through reason are nothing but efforts to understand, and the mind, in so far as it uses reason, adjudges nothing as profitable to itself except that which conduces to understanding. This effort to understand is the primary and sole foundation of virtue. That which actually conduces to understanding is certainly good and that which can prevent us from understanding is certainly bad. And thus proceeding, the knowledge of God is the highest good of the mind and to know God is the highest virtue. Summing, up therefore, the more perfect we make our intellect, the more virtue we are endowed with. There is no rational life without intelligence. The way to happiness and blessedness for man consists in being guided by reason to adequately conceive himself and all things.

In so far as an object agrees with our nature, it is necessarily good. But men, as long as they are subject to passion do not agree in nature. A passion-ridden man is changeable and inconsistent. But when men are guided by reason alone, they necessarily agree with one another. There is no single thing in Nature which is more profitable to man than a man who lives according to reason. The highest good of those who follow after virtue is common to all and all can equally enjoy it. (31-36 Sch.)

Thus, Spinoza's ethical doctrines are, (a) self-maintenance as the foundation of virtue, (b) intelligence as the foundation of ethical judgment and (c) the common nature and interests of men as the ground of social ethics. We see how Spinoza, through his artful method, has reconciled individual good with the social good. Herbert Spencer, in his *Data of Ethics*, pictures the society as an organism in which each man is a member. The end is pleasure but it consists in the health of the social organism. Spencer also visualizes a day when there will be no conflict between individual and social interests. Spinoza, two centuries before Spencer, also wrote that man and society did not clash with each other. However, like Spencer, he did not deduce his ethical sanction from the gladiatorial theory of the universe. His ground of argument was the life of reason. We destroy one another because we are affected by passions. Reason only tells us that all men are one in interest and man is at his best in society. As Sidgwick remarks, the wise man is a 'cosmopolitical animal.' Did Spinoza not anticipate Kropotkin when he wrote, "Let satirists scoff at human affairs as much as they please, let theologians denounce them, and let the melancholy praise as much as they can a life rude and without refinement, despising men and admiring brutes, men will nevertheless find out that by mutual help they can much more easily procure the things they need, and that it is only by their united strength they can avoid the dangers which everywhere threaten them." Man has not to look above for redemption from sin; he has not to bow down to invoke the pleasure of deities to grant him a smooth sailing in life, but he is to act by reason, here in this world, amidst the human assembly surrounding him. Man is man's best friend, his redeemer. 'Man is a God to Man.'

Everything, which we desire and do, of which we are the cause in so far as we possess and idea of God, Spinoza refers to religion. This religious spirit, actuated in the life of a man guided by reason, he calls piety. And to him, it is an honorable thing to practice the life of piety in the community of fellowmen.

In ethics, Spinoza often resembles the Stoics of Greece. A life according to reason, which consists in self-preservation, was the Stoic doctrine. Both treat the social character of man as a fact of common experience. Their self-preservation does not imply selfishness. Both stress the active nature of virtue. But Spinoza, unlike the Stoics, made his ethical code free from all sorts of teleology.

Spinoza's man is a strong man. He frees him from all gloomy and sad superstition, which stands in the way of human happiness. "No God and no human being, except an envious one, is delighted by my impotence or my trouble, or esteems as any virtue in us, tears, sighs, fears and other things of this kind, which are signs of mental impotence; on the contrary, the greater the joy with which we are affected, the greater the perfection to which we pass thereby, that is to say, the more do we partake of the divine nature. To make use of things, therefore, and to delight in them as much as possible (provided we do not disgust ourselves with them, which is not delighting in them), is the part of a wise man. It is the part of a wise man, I say, to refresh and invigorate himself with moderate and pleasant eating and drinking, with sweet scents and the beauty of green plants, with ornaments, with music, with sports, with the theatre and with all things of this kind which one man can enjoy without hurting another." One wonders whether he reads Epicurus in these lines. We are surprised to think that Spinoza, himself an outlaw from friends and society, could so clearly understand man and his needs. He avoided the two extremes. On the one hand his was not the Cyrenaic[49] theory of 'no regret for the past, no trouble for future, but to surrender oneself with a careless abandon to the present.' He did never take life for a 'fretful child that must be played with till it falls to sleep.' On the other hand also, he never preached asceticism, nor a way of sadistic self-mortification like those early Christian monks who said that the soul was most healthy in a sick body. In this respect

49. This refers to the hedonistic world-view of Epicurus.

he was averse to the Stoics, who tortured the body to elevate the mind and for such practice, prescribed a bed of hand planks without any coverings and a single tunic of rough cloth that was a torture to the skin. Of those ascetics, who forsake the world to realize virtue in dead solitude, Spinoza speaks with his usual taunt that "they are injurious both to themselves and to others, so that many of them through an excess of impatience and a false zeal for religion, prefer living with brutes rather than amongst men; just as boys or youths, unable to endure with equanimity the rebukes of their parents, fly to the army."[50] Spinoza follows the golden mean. His track is not for brutes who live by mere sensations, or for the life-forsakes who flee away from the rigour of life. It is for men, strong men, joined in society. In fact Spinoza identifies virtue and power.[51]

Spinoza's man has to practise the life of virtue here in society where multinatured affects tend to sweep away the minds of men. Hence the man of reason has to discriminate between different affects and see which of them are really conducive for the preservation of his being and to what extent. The same affect, we have already seen, can be both efficacious and harmful to us accordingly as we pursue it. For our safe sailing, Spinoza makes a keen investigation of some of the affects and ascertains to what extent they are helpful to live a virtuous life.

Our end is joy and it comes by living a life of reason; in other words, a virtuous life. Joy is directly good and sorrow is directly evil. Cheerfulness can never be excessive but is always good; melancholy, on the contrary, is always evil. When pleasurable excitement becomes excessive, it is then an evil, and pain may also be good in so far as it can restrain an excess of pleasurable excitement. Love and desire also may be excessive. They can also be tainted by selfishness. He, who strives to make others love what he himself loves, is selfish. Hatred can never be good. Envy, mockery, contempt, anger, revenge and the other affects that emanate from hatred are evil. (By hatred, Spinoza warns us, he means hatred towards men only). But hatred is increased by reciprocal hatred and, on the other hand, can be extinguished by love, so that hatred passes into love. So the man of reason tries, as far

---

50. Ethic: p. 244.
51. Ethic: IV. Def. 8.

as possible, to repay the hatred, anger or contempt of others towards himself with love or generosity. He, who wishes to avenge injuries by hating in return, does indeed live miserably. But he, who, on the contrary, strives to drive out hatred by love, fights joyfully and confidently, with equal ease resisting one man or a number of men, and needing scarcely any assistance from fortune. Those whom he conquers yield gladly, not from defect of strength, but from an increase of it. (41-46) These truths, Spinoza concludes, all follow plainly from the definitions alone of love and intellect.

Over-estimation, pity, humility and pride are in themselves evils and only show the despondency and weakness of man. Spinoza calls these and other like affects, evils in so far as he attends to human profit alone; but the laws of Nature have regard for the common order of Nature of which man is a part. He considers human affects and their properties precisely as he considers other natural objects. To him, the affects of man, if they do not show his power, show, at least, the power and workmanship of Nature. The man who has properly understood that everything follows from the necessity of the divine nature and comes to pass according to the eternal laws and rules of Nature, will, in truth, discover nothing which is worthy of hatred, laughter or contempt, nor will he pity anyone; but so far as human virtue is able, he will endeavour to do well, as we say, and rejoice. The life of reason that he lives will give him the highest self-satisfaction.

Any action is called evil in so far as it arises from our being affected with hatred or some evil effect (45 cor). But one and the same action is sometimes good and sometimes evil. Enunciating it in its proper form, "To all actions to which we are determined by an affect which is a passion, we may, without the affect, be determined by reason. (59) Spinoza makes the point clearer by an illustration from common life. The action of striking physically constitutes raising one's arm, closing the hand and forcibly moving the hand downwards, and thus it is considered a virtue. But if an agitated man does the same things, we call it striking and call it bad. Hence, we see that the one and the same action can be joined to different images of things. And every desire, born of passion would be of no use if men could be guided by reason. Reason can sublimate all our passions to which we may be affected.

A desire, which springs from reason, can never be in excess. Reason annihilates the preference of time, that is, when we are guided by reason; we are equally affected by the idea of an object, whether the idea be that of something future, past or present. The man of reason follows good directly and avoids evil indirectly, but never does so out of fear. His reason tells him that his good can be increased as far as he possesses adequate ideas and that all evil originates from only inadequate ideas. Goodness and adequacy being our only criteria of ideas, when we follow reason, we will always, of two good things, follow the greater good, notwithstanding whether it belongs to the past, the present or the future. Quite unlike when swayed by passions, our reason will tell us to do without the present good for the sake of a greater future good.

Spinoza ends the chapter with some more explanations of the qualities of a free man. The difference between a man of reason and one who is passion-led can be easily deduced. The latter, whether he wills it or not, does those things of which he is ignorant, but the former does the will of no one but himself and does only those things which he knows are of greatest importance in life and which he, therefore, desires above all things. The latter is a slave and the former, a free man. The free man thinks nothing less than of death and his wisdom is not a meditation upon death but upon life. [This last sentence is borrowed from Plato and reads so similarly with Goethe's *memento vivere* or 'remember to live'.]

If men were born free, they would form no cónception of good and evil so long as they were free. These free men are alone grateful to one another not as from a matter of business, nor from a snare, but from a genuine spirit of gratitude. They never act deceitfully but always honorably. All these good qualities have been bestowed upon the free men as far as they have fortitude or the strength of mind. Fortitude will lead its possessor to hate no one, be angry with no one, not to envy, nor to despise anybody and never to be proud. He will consider above everything that all things follow from the necessity of the divine nature, and that, consequently, whatever he thinks injurious and evil, and whatever seems to be impious, dreadful, unjust or wicked, arises from this, that he conceives things in a disturbed, mutilated and confused fashion. For this reason, his chief effort will be to conceive things as they are in themselves, and to remove the hindrances to true knowledge, such as hatred, anger, envy etc. and so he will endeavour, as much as possible, to do well and rejoice. (73. Sc.)

(g) Deliverance of Man

"*To you I declare this holy mystery,*
There is nothing nobler than humanity."—

The Māhabhārata, (XII-300-20)

"*Love makes all things equal....*
The spirit of the worm beneath the soul
In love and worship, blends itself with God."

—Epipsychidion, 128-29

In the fifth part, remarks a student of Spinoza, leaving the indicative mood, Spinoza passes on to imperative and ventures on daring flights. All through the ages Spinoza has remained a riddle to the speculators' mind, at least as far as this last part of *Ethic* is concerned. Let us see, in sketchy summarizing how far Spinoza has genuinely proved his case and also whether he has exactly said what he meant.

The fifth part of the *Ethic*, its author says, concerns the method or way which leads to liberty. In the part that preceded, we have been acquainted with the passions that entangle the mind in thralldom and also what it is like to be a free man. In this part Spinoza will treat the power of reason, showing how much reason itself can control the affects and then what is freedom of mind or blessedness. And then we will, in fact, know how much stronger the wise man is than the ignorant.

At the outset, Spinoza reiterates his stand about the power of the human mind. He proves that the latter is only a mode and is susceptible to countless external powers. Vindicating his own stand, he refutes the standing theories about the absolute power of the human mind. It was a common fallacy with the philosophers of the time that the soul occupies a corner of its own in the body and there from, exercises free will. The idea had got impetus from the soul-atom theory, the survival of the wornout metaphysics of Democritus. And Descartes, who was so much physiologically biased, affirmed that the soul or mind is united specially to a certain part of the brain called the pineal gland, which the mind, by exercising the will, is able to move in different ways. This gland, Descartes supposed, is suspended in the middle of the brain in such a manner that it can be moved by the least stir of the animal spirits.

Each volition was the result of only a certain motion of this gland, from which it was assumed that the mind, if rightly directed, can have control over the passions. Spinoza welds his argument against these wrong theorists who devise seats and dwelling places of the soul' and in so doing, 'excite our laughter and disgust'. (II 35 Sc). Spinoza justifies his trenchancy when he says, "I can hardly wonder enough that a philosopher who firmly resolved to make no deduction except from self-evident principles and to affirm nothing but what he clearly and distinctly perceived, and who blamed all the schoolmen because they desired to explain obscure matters by occult qualities, should accept a hypothesis more occult than any occult quality." Hence our mind has no hegemony over our affections and the extent and the nature of the authority which it can have over them, is only as far as the intelligence we possess.

The truths that follow, are delivered in their due order; by presenting the one, Spinoza prepares the readers' mind for the next. The order is, (a) the excellence of understanding in liberating the mind from all our affections, (b) the excellence of love culminating in the *amor intellectualis Dei* with the help of the third kind of knowledge and (c) the divine glory of the mind resultant of this beatitude or blessedness.

The Spinozistic interpretation of an affect, it must be remembered, is no positive mental phenomena which comes, as it were, from outside and takes possession of the mind. An affect is a confused idea. Falsity also is no positive quality, it is only the absence of truth, it is a privation. In the terms of the *Vaishésika* school of logic, falsity is but the *Atyantābhāba* of truth. Spinoza has previously asserted that falsehood consists in the privation of knowledge which is involved by inadequate and confused ideas (II 35). All that is confusion can stick to us only as long as we have not understood a thing properly and fully. Our power of intelligence can show us in and across the screen of passions. As possessing this power over the patchy and flashy notions, intelligence has been described by Spinoza as the mind's 'eternal part'. This eternal part corresponds to the 'Active reason' of Aristotle. Let us mark the way in which Spinoza proceeds. "If we detach an emotion of the mind or affect from the thought of an external cause and connect it with other thought, then the love or hatred towards the external cause and the fluctuations of the mind which arise from these affects will be destroyed." "An affect which is a passion, ceases to be a passion as soon as we form a clear and distinct idea of it." "There is no affection of the body of which we cannot form some clear and distinct conception." (Prop. 1, 2, 3) The corollary annotates, "Hence it follows, there is no affect of which we can not have some clear and distinct conception." And we hear the optimistic note that everyone has the power, partly at least, if not absolutely, of understanding clearly and distinctly himself and his affects, and consequently of suffering less from them. So it devolves upon every aspirant to strive to acquire a clear and distinct knowledge, as far as possible, of each affect and to strive so that the affect may be separated from the thought of the external cause. No affect can be conceived of but those conceived along with the idea of an external thing. And when this idea of the external thing is obliterated from the mind, for pure conceptions of them only remains, and as a mathematician deals with the various things which come as instances to his problems, we will also be able to conceive the idea of the affects without being the least affected.

A thing is never good or bad in itself, but is so far as we adequately or inadequately approach it. We are but betrayed by our own understanding. The one attitude of adoration can be turned to love or lust. All our appetites, and desires are passions, only in so far as they arise from inadequate ideas and are classed as virtues whenever begotten by adequate ones. So, Spinoza concludes, the only accessible remedies consists in a true knowledge of the affects since the mind has no other power than that of thinking and forming adequate ideas (III 3).

The destiny of the soul depends on the direction of its affections. Writes Spinoza, "If it (the soul or mind) remains united with the perishable body alone, then it must also perish. But if it becomes united with some other thing, which is unchangeable and abides, then it can not but be unchangeable and abide.[52] From this 'landing place', let us proceed to what he says in his mature work: "An affect towards

52. *Short Treatise*, Book II.Ch 23.

an object which we do not imagine as necessary, possible or contingent, but which we simply imagine, is the greatest of all." [Imagining a thing simply means nothing else than imagining it free of (Demon V 5), and a free thing, in Spinozistic sense, means nothing but that, of whose cause of existence we are ignorant.] But in so far as the mind understands all things as necessary, that is, as determined to existence and action by an infinite chain of causes (I 28), so far has it greater power over the affects, or suffers less from them" (5, 6).

How to understand things as necessary? Spinoza's answer is, by arranging our affects. Every moment upon the canvas of mind, are crowded innumerable affects of innumerable nature and they leave the mind in helpless bewilderment. We hate many things, we love many others, some cause sorrow in us and some cause joy. They come and go, grip the mind as long as they stay and sweep it in multifarious ways. The way out is to come to them with the poise that our power of understanding gives us, and arrange them in such a way that they are connected with or related to one another. Hence, as long as the natural endeavour of the mind is not hindered, or as long as it possesses the power of forming clear and distinct ideas, so long do we posses the power of arranging and connecting of the affections of the body according to the order of the intellect (10).

By this power of properly arranging and connecting the affections, we can prevent ourselves from being tossed by their evil effects. But things are always easier said than done. Though arranged and connected, affects can with less difficulty be restrained than those uncertain and unsettled, it yet requires practice, translating this spirit to life by daily practice. To the Eastern student of philosophy, it will not be very difficult to understand its import. The rites and rituals, daily oblations and prayers have a very highly esteemed place in the practice of *Sadhānā*. We get them in the sermons of Shankara who prescribes them for mental purification, for *Chittasūddhi* as he calls it. The *Geeta* also lays so much stress on *Abhyāsa* and *Vairāgya*. Here, we also find lack of perfect knowledge of our affects, which is to conceive a right rule of life or some maxims (dogma) of life-to commit these latter to memory and constantly to apply them to the particular cases which frequently meet us in life, so that our imagination may be widely affected by them and they always be ready to hand." (10. Schol) Taking an example, we know the rule that hatred should not be returned by hatred, but love. We may not be strong enough to practise this maxim at the first instance. To be at home with the rule so as to follow it when required we must "think over and meditate upon the common injuries inflicted by men, and consider how and in what way they may best be repelled by generosity; thus by frequent mental connection of the two images of injury and generosity we will have the latter at hand in case an injury is done to us. If we also have at hand the law of our own true profit and good which follows from joining in friendship with fellowmen and remember that the highest peace of mind arises from a right rule of life (iv 52) and also that man, like other things, acts according to the necessity of nature, then the injury or the hatred which usually arises from that necessity will occupy but the least part of the imagination and will be easily overcome." And what are the means of cultivating the strength of mind? "We must reflect," Spinoza says, "in the same way for the purpose of getting rid of fear" that is to say, we must often enumerate and imagine the common dangers of life, and think upon the manner in which they can be overcome by presence of mind and courage. How near does it come to the *Pratipaksha Bhābanā* of the Indian Yogi which commands us to think of courage to rid fear, of love to rid hatred!

Life is not a constant battle with hostile forces, nor is it only hiding oneself away with eternal alertness from the forces of evil. Life is, above all, to be lived. Living is a positive duty and hence we must, before everything else, have a positive outlook on life. Our life is neither a mere store-house of ossified character-moulds, nor a negative existence by moral inhibitions. In the words of the Indian sages of yore, life is *Dharma.* And this *Dharma* is to be observed by following what is good, but never by merely withdrawing oneself from evil. As Spinoza warns us, "in the ordering of our thoughts and images, we must always look to those qualities which in each thing are good, so that we may be determined to action always by an affect of joy." For if we see that we pursue glory too eagerly, the best way to rid this passion is to think on its proper use, for what end it is to be followed, but never to think upon its abuse and vanity. Indeed, it is true that those covet glory the most who are the most profuse in declaiming against its abuse and vanity of the world. Those who speak about life with spite are the very worms who would like to stick to it under any circumstance. Therefore Spinoza advices those who will assist people to live a life of the highest good, that they will "avoid referring to the vices of men and will take care only sparingly to speak of human impotence, while [they] will talk largely on human virtue or power, and of the way by which it may be made perfect, so that men, being moved not by fear or aversion, but solely by the affect of joy may endeavour, as far as possible, to live the life of reason." This recalls St.Paul's injunction, "whatsoever things are honorable, whatsoever things are just, whatsoever things are pure, whatsoever things are lovely, whatsoever things are of good report, think on these things." And how close it is with the spirited advice of Swami Vivekananda, whom Rolland also calls the St. Paul of India, when he writes, "Never hear anyone in private, talking ill of another?" Spinoza concludes, "He who desires to govern his affects and appetites from a love of liberty alone, will strive as much as he can, to know virtues and their causes, and to fill his mind with that joy which springs from a true knowledge of them."

This mind, full of joy, is what William James means by the 'healthy-minded temperament'. Repentance and remorse have no positive place in life. Salvation is never for the sick soul. 'The best repentance is to be up and act for righteousness', and forget that one ever had relations with sin!

"Spinoza's philosophy", James continues, "has this sort of healthy-mindedness woven into the heart of it and this has been one secret of its fascination. Spinoza categorically condemns repentance. When men make mistakes, he says, 'one might perhaps expect gnawing of conscience and repentance to help to bring them on the right path, and might thereupon conclude that these affections are good things. Yet when we look at the matter closely, we shall find that not only are they not good, but on the contrary, deleterious and evil passions. For it is manifest that we can always get along better by reason and love of truth than by worry of conscience and remorse. Harmful are these and evil, in as much as they form a particular kind of sadness; and the disadvantages of sadness', he continues, 'I have already proved and shown that we should strive to keep it from our life. Just so we should endeavour, since uneasiness of conscience and remorse are of this kind of complexion, to free and shun these states of mind.[53]

53. William James, *The Varieties of Religious Experience*, p. 125.

Reason only conceives things in their essence and as necessary, in other words, conceives them as a part of the order of existence, that is, of God. So our mind, in so far as it is guided by the dictates of reason, can regard all the affections of the body or the images of things as related to the idea of God. The perfect and distinct knowledge of things is the way to perfect joy and hence the man, who distinctly understands, necessarily loves God. With our better understanding, our love for God goes on increasing. As God is the most perfect being and is the eternal order of both essence and existence, he is the mind's dearest possession. He is free from passions, untouched by joy or sorrow. In fact, He loves no one and hates no one because the affects of love and hate always presuppose the idea of an external thing, and there is nothing external to God. No one can hate God. He who loves God cannot strive that God should love him in return. This love of God cannot be defiled either by the affect of envy or jealousy, but is more strengthened, the more people we imagine to be connected with God by the same bond of love (18-20).

Recapitulating what Spinoza has affirmed about the power of understanding, we see that the power of the mind over the affects consists (1) in the knowledge itself of the affects, (2) in the separation by the mind of the affects from the thought of an external cause, which we imagine confusedly (3) in duration for which the affections which are related to objects we understand surpass those related to the objects conceived in a mutilated or confused manner, (4) in the multitude of causes by which the affections which are related to the common properties of things or to God are nourished, or the order in which the mind can arrange its affects and connect them with one another.

One wonders at Spinoza's treatment of love in the last three propositions quoted above. It rises to such a pitch that it seems to smack of the love of a man to a personal God. But as we know, all attempts at anthropomorphism were foreign to Spinoza. The truth is, his approach was only that of love, the love towards a higher thing, towards an object that is less transitory. Many passages can be quoted from more than one of his books. "Our sorrows and misfortunes mainly proceed from too much love towards an object which is subject to many changes, and which we can never possess."[54] "All our happiness and unhappiness depends solely on the quality of the object on which our love is fixed. [..] Love towards an object eternal and infinite feeds the mind with joy that is pure, with no tinge of sadness."[55] Such is the life of 'thoughts immortal and divine' of which Plato and Aristotle also speak." He whose heart has been set on the love of learning and of true wisdom, must without fail have thoughts that are immortal and divine, if he lay hold on truth: and so far as it lies in human nature to possess immortality, (in this higher sense), he lacks nothing thereof."[56]

What is the God of Spinoza? It is Nature, the external order of essence and existence of things. So when we realize that all our affects follow from the eternal necessity of the order of things, we sense the vastness of this order; in other words, we know God. And as all adequate knowledge leads not to sorrow, but joy, to understand God is to love God. This love is of no utilitarian character; nay, it emanates from the love of knowledge and the joy of liberty, resulting from finding oneself in an ineffaceable order. This love is self-originated and wants nothing in return. A mathematician expects nothing from a problem because he has solved it out. The fact that he has solved it is in itself a joy to him. "Religious life is spiritual certainty offering us strength and solace in the hour of need and sorrow. It is the conviction that love and justice are at the heart of the universe, that the spirit which gives rise to man, will further its perfection. [..] It is so utterly indifferent to what happens to the little self and so completely taken up by the life of spirit. This is perhaps the significance of Spinoza's great saying that he who loves God can not want that God should love him in return. Highest love does not expect any return, reward or recompense."[57] Or as Rabindranath has put it, "What is the price of the freedom of consciousness? It is to give oneself away."[58] A soul emancipated never wants anything in return. It rejoices in giving away. The Upanisad says: *téna tyakténa*

54. Ethic. V. 20, Schol.
55. Int. Emendations, Sec. 9-10.
56. Plato, Timaeus. p. 90.
57. Radhakrishnan, The Religion We Need, p. 27.
58. Sādhanā, p. 19.

bhunjeethāh, ma grdha ' Thou shalt gain by giving away; thou shalt not covet.'

From here, Spinoza takes a leap which is, according to Pollock, 'the singular and difficult part of the book.' After dealing with all the remedies for our affectations, Spinoza passes to the 'consideration of those matters which appertain to the duration of the mind without relation to the body'. As long as the body exists, all our thoughts are woven round this life only. Entangled in body, the mind becomes deluded to think everything as actual as it happens in time. But when, with the growth of our power of understanding, we attribute all the affects to God, Nature or the eternal order, our sense of time is changed. And if God, as we have seen before, is the eternal essence of things, the mind, thus illumined by reason, knows all things as following from God, or, in the famous Spinozistic phrase, knows them '*sub specie aeternitatis*'. When Spinoza says that the human mind can not be destroyed with the body, but something of it remains which is eternal, many critics suppose him as affirming pre-existence and the survival of consciousness after death. If body and mind are the only two intelligible attributes of God, equally representing his essence, how is it that a portion of mind becomes eternal while the body perishes? Spinoza's explanation is that 'we feel and know by experience that we are eternal.' Even granted that we feel in us a sense of eternity, why can not the body be eternal along with the mind? As no clarification is forthcoming, Spinoza remains inscrutable at this point. Still it can be said in his defence that henceforward he brings to view things with the third kind of knowledge and therefore his visions also begin to change in their nature. A mystic's vision can not be tested by ordinary cognition. Let us have faith in the escort though he follows a different track, then only can we share with him the view of the ocean of experiences to which we are led in.

The theory of seeing things *sub specie aeternitatis* was Spinoza's glory. Everything follows from Him who is the All, everything is in Him who manifests Himself from the necessity of His own existence. He is revealed through me, through you, through everything. A perfect understanding of the particular things also means understanding God. The world is in God, God is the world. The perfect knowledge is this knowledge of the All. This same truth was also felt by the Rishis of India when they sang,-*yo bai bhūmā sūkham nālpé sūkhamasti bhūmaiba sūkham bhūmātwéba bijignyāsitabya*

'That which is immensity is felicity; there is no felicity in exiguity. Immensity alone is felicity; Immensity alone is worthy of enquiry.' (Chhandogya: 7/23) This 'knowing everything under the form of eternity' is also very akin to the Stoic idea of 'welcoming every event'. Knowing that they all follow from God, we would be relieved of much of our sorrows, Spinoza asserts, we would view things *sub specie aeternitatis*. Often we suffer by bringing in too much of ourselves to any incident. Being a little more objective would surely save us from many aches and agonies. Tagore hints at the same idea in one of his passages by citing an incident from his daily life, "Once I was getting terrible pain from scorpion-bite. Suddenly the thought came to me, that it was not I, but a certain poet, Rabindranath by name, who was suffering. I began to look upon myself as a separate entity. I could then see, as it were from a distance, that this man named Rabindranath was having pain. At once all my pain was gone,—I forgot everything."

What is meant by intuition, the third kind of knowledge? "The highest effort of the mind and its highest virtue is to understand things by the third kind of knowledge, from which arises in man's power of knowing by reason, the second kind as previously mentioned. Our rational self arises to the intuitional self and by this power the mind conceives the essence of the body *sub specie aeternitatis*" (25-30) Martinue calls intuition "at once higher and ulterior which Spinoza describes in terms of tantalizing and perhaps studied obscurity." He doubts if Spinoza had a "perfect self-understanding respecting the nature and the scope of intuitive knowledge. A certain embarrassment is apparent in his exposition of it."[59] In the second part of *Ethic*, (40, Schol) Intuition is defined as the third kind of knowledge 'which advances from the adequate idea of the essence of things.' Spinoza calls this intuition (*scientia intuitiva*' and like Plato, distinguishes ratio, whose movement is regressive) from effect to cause, from variety of unity from intuition whose movement is attributes of God progressive, which proceeds from the adequate idea of certain to an adequate knowledge of the nature of things. Spinoza was not the first among the philosophers to admit intuition as the highest form of knowledge. Jacob Boehme meant the same form when he said,

59. Martinue's, p. 159.

"When I thus write, the spirit of a great wonderful recognition is dictating to me." Keats also speaks of a 'good genius' presiding over him as he writes.[60] Tagore also refers to an unknown hand which leads him on in his writing. Hugo de St.Victor, a mystic of the middle ages, says that the inner revelation of man is the highest form of recognition. Fichte's 'intellectual intuition' comes very near to Spinoza's *scientia intuitiva.* Fichte says that the unity of the sensuous and the supersensuous worlds cannot be reached by a psychological or logical train of reasoning but by a process of 'intellectual intuition.' For Bergson, intuition was the creative consciousness that leads us to the very inwardness of life.

In India, intuition was known as *dibyadristi. Only* with the 'third eye', we can get the knowledge of the essence of things. It is immediate, as Spinoza also interpreted it. As Rabindranath puts it, 'it is not mere knowledge as science, but it is a perception of the soul by the soul.'[61] So it should not be thought that Spinoza made his last part 'laboriously enigmatical' by allowing into it this third kind of knowledge. It is the stage par excellence that comes in the wake of our cognitive evolution. It is not magic, nor is it another name for trance. Quoting Sir Radhakrishnan, "Intuition is not a sensual skill or an emotional debauch. [..] If intuition is unsupported by intellect, it will lapse into self-satisfied obscurantism. Intuition assumes that continuity and unity of all experience. An intellectual search for the ultimate cause may lead us to an idea of God."[62]

By intuition, the mind knows everything, not *sub specie boni*, but *sub specie aeternitatis*. And knowing this, it necessarily has a knowledge of God and is conceived through Him. In whatever we understand by intuition, we delight; and our delight is accompanied with the idea of God as its cause. From this, springs the intellectual love of God. Perfect knowledge engenders perfect joy at the idea of God, that is, the love of God, not in so far as we imagine Him as present, but in so far as we understand that He is eternal and this is what Spinoza calls the *amor intellectualis Dei* or the intellectual love of God. This love, as it is fixed on God, who is eternal, is also eternal.

---

60. Letter to Haydon, 10th May, 1817.
61. Sadhana, p. 8.
62. *My Search For Truth*, p. 29.

Amor intellectualis Dei has been subject to stringent criticisms from various standpoints. Critics who regard Spinoza as a transcendental dogmatist take for granted that Spinoza dogmatises about the eternity of the mind, and about substance and the attributes. Others hold that his theory is a doctrine of personal immortality in the ordinary sense, only stated in an unusual way and supported by artificial reasoning (This we have already falsified). Others suppose that Spinoza did not clearly know his own meaning, or he could not say what he meant or he deliberately said things he did not mean. Let us also stop here to examine the consistency of Spinoza's developments. By the intellectual love of God, the mind passes to the highest perfection. (V. 27) Going back with Spinoza, highest perfection is highest reality and also activity, (vi Preface) and activity is always accompanied with joy. Thus reduced, the *amor Dei* is that state of the highest kind of joy which follows from the knowledge of the highest perfection.

Spinoza has given us his three orders of knowledge, the one excelling the other in ascending order or merit. The first stage is that of quick reactions to external stimuli, giving us only inadequate ideas. The second is the life of science and freedom or the stage of reason. The highest reason gives us fortitude and strength of mind. The third ushers in that state, when the mind can perceive immediately. Our instincts become intuition and emotion becomes action. Intuition is not discursive, that is, going from part to part, but it follows from the wholeness of nature. And this stage brings us to *amor Dei*. It is the consequence of complete self-knowledge, not of all knowledge. The God infinite, is not a spiritual encyclopedia. Infinite does not mean here so much an extent as a quality of being. As Ratner says," The intellectual love of God does not demand, as a basis, a knowledge of the cosmic concatenation of things. [..] It depends solely upon a knowledge of the order of Nature, upon a knowledge of the infinite and eternal essence of God."[63]

Spinoza has been called a mystic by some critics. Pollock remarks that but for his scientific training in the school of Descartes, Spinoza would have been a mystic. To know oneself as a part of God, is, according to him, the highest stage in realization. 'I am in God and

---

63. Introduction to 'Philosophy of Spinoza', Modern Library 60, p. LXI.

God in me' is also the essence of Indian philosophy. '*Ayamātma Brahma* (Māndūkya)', (Chhāndogya) and '*Aham Brahmāsmi*' are its many illustrations. The Isha Upanisad says, '*tadantarasya sarbasya*' He is within all this'.

Spinoza started with God and ends with God. With his intellectual love, he knows the God whom he had assumed at the outset. For this tendency of going beyond the power of reason in the case of many philosophers, many scientists call them the 'priests of the second order'. There has also been an attempt at reconciling mysticism with skepticism. Aubury Moore remarks, "Philosophy does not become mystical and take refuge in flight until it abandons all hope of converting the world, when effort is useless, the mind idealizes inaction and seeks a metaphysical basis for it. For mysticism and skepticism flourish in the same atmosphere, though in different soils; both though in different ways, implying the abandonment of the rational problem."[64] The die-hard rationalist has this paranoiac habit of calling everything skeptical, all that he does not understand. We have seen that Spinoza did never abandon the rational problems, nor did he escape to the 'waters of no more pain'. He never divorces reason from passion. According to Gunn, his *amor Dei* is a synthesis of feeling and intellect. It is based on the Socratic 'Know Thyself' and upon a knowledge *de Rerum Natura*, that is, of the universe and man's relation to it. Ratner makes it clearer when he says, "The great religious significance of Spinoza's doctrine of the intellectual love of God is that it establishes religion upon knowledge and not upon ignorance. The virtue of the mind is clearly and distinctly to understand, not ignorantly to believe. There is no conflict between science and religion, religion is based upon science. There is a conflict only between science and superstition."

Spinoza reconciled his perfect knowledge with love, the nature of which remains still inscrutable to many critics. They often look at it with worldly estimations of sensual love and affirm that it suffers from inconsistencies. There is also a theory that mysticism and sensualism vary only in degree, but not in kind. Max Muller says, 'there is nothing in the faith that was not in the senses.' Psychologists like Jung have vehemently proved that all types of religiosity are

---

64. Introduction to *Chuang Tzu* translated by H.A. Giles.

replete with eroticism. Arnold Ruge, the theologian, has stated that 'mysticism is theological voluptuousness and voluptuousness is practical mysticism.' Both are born in the emotions, in the deeply felt need to perpetuate the self. The intensification of these motives leads to mysticism in religion and voluptuousness in love. According to Melamed, Spinoza's *amor Dei* is only erotic mysticism.

Patches of events from the lives of mystics as St. Teresa, Lady Julian and Miss Underhill often suggest eroticism to many critics. The songs of the Vaishnava lore also affirm the relation of a lover with his beloved. Modern psychologists tell us that the history of mysticism is the history of neurosis. Then what is the difference between eroticism and mysticism. The latter lands us in a totally different mental attitude. Eroticism only means the instinct of lust crying out for assuagement. But the other is a waking up and a realization. It is a state that comes when man has done away with all lust and particularity. It wants to sustain itself by giving itself away. This can never be taken for as a next development of eroticism. As Rabindranath writes, 'Love is another name for perfect comprehension'[65] and a man attains his freedom and fulfillment in it. It is a joy to find oneself joined in essence to the world, it is knowing God to be supreme joy: *raso bai sah* 'the infinite is love itself' as the ancient Rishis of India had known it.

When the individual mind attains the state of *amor Dei*, it becomes a part of God, it finds itself in God. The one mingles with the All as a river with the ocean. The essence of God in each man confluences with the infinite essence. This is what Spinoza means when he says that God loves Himself with an infinite intellectual love. In proposition 36, he writes, "The intellectual love of the mind towards God is the very love with which He loves himself, not in so far as He is infinite, but in so far as He can be explained through the essence of the human mind considered under the form of eternity; that is to say, the intellectual love of the mind towards God is part of the infinite love with which God loves Himself." Spinoza's words here come very near to those of Hallaj, the mystic—philosopher of Persia who wrote, "I am God, I am He whom I love, and He whom I love is

---

65. Sadhana, p. 15.

I. We are two spirits dwelling in one body. If you see me, you see Him, and seeing Him, you see us both."

Herein consists our salvation and blessedness, in the constant and eternal love towards God. The more this kind of love grows in us, the less we suffer from evil affects and the less we fear death. Our body, the emblem of our perishable existence gradually becomes a possession of no consequence. Though, in the beginning, Spinoza has established the equality of body and mind, both following from Substance, in this part he makes the mind superior. Spinoza, the mystic, has superseded Spinoza, the metaphysician. Or it may signify that when our mind begins to view God in everything, it ceases to distinguish between the attributes, which are but the aspects of the one Substance and only the *natura naturans* is present before it. In Prop. 36 Schol, Spinoza writes: "[..] although I have shown generally in the first part that all things, and consequently, also the human mind, depend upon God, both with regard to existence and essence, yet that demonstration, although legitimate and placed beyond the possibility of a doubt, does not, nevertheless, so affect our mind as a proof from the essence itself of any individual object which, we say, depends upon God."

Blessedness is an end in itself, not simply a means. It is, in itself, a precious possession, not a mere expedient. It is "not the reward of virtue but is virtue itself; nor do we delight in blessedness because we restrain our lusts; but, on the contrary, because we delight in it, therefore are we able to restrain them" (42)

Thus Spinoza comes to the end of his book. "I have finished everything I wished to explain concerning the power of the mind over the affects and concerning its liberty." We have seen how strong the wise man is, who is never moved in his mind, and always enjoys the true peace of the soul. He brings the chapter to a close with an austerity that is saint-like. "If the way, as I have shown, leads hither seem very difficult, it can nevertheless be found. It must indeed be difficult since it is so seldom discovered; for if salvation lay ready at hand and could be discovered without great labour, how could it be possible that it should be neglected almost by everybody?" And last is struck the most optimistic note for every worthy aspirant: "But all noble things are as difficult as they are rare." Does not the *Katha Upanishad* sing with the same passionate zeal when it says:

Men of illumination say that the path of realization is very sharp

Like like the end of the razor and is very difficult to traverse; but still ye arise, awake and stop not till the goal is reached (1/3/14)

(h) Spinoza and Theology

I shall even go to the length of rejecting the divinity of the most ancient shastras, if they do not appeal to my reason.
[..] one should never take anything for gospel truth
even if it comes from a Mahatma, unless it
appeals to both his head and heart.

—*Māhatmā Gāndhi*, Harijan, 17.3.46.

The Jewish society of the 17th century lay immersed in magic and miracle, in sorcery and superstition. These devotees of the Old Testament thought God as Father, Creator and Protector. The metaphysics of the Jews was nothing but religion and revelation. Jehovah, the heavenly Father was the tribal Deity, struggling and battling all the time. He was merciful to those who appeased Him and kept Him in good humour. But to the least defier, he sent this wrath. Baruch Spinoza was the first Jew to develop a passion for the Absolute and, as a consequence, was driven out of the Synagogue. And if he had lived in the first century instead of the 17th, May Sinclair remarks, "the Jews would have crucified him."[66]

The contemporary society was the worst sufferer from bibliolatry. The Protestants had substituted the belief in an infallible book for that in an infallible church. As has been protested by Lessing, "O Luther, thou hast delivered us from the bondage of the Papacy, who will deliver us from the slavery of the letter?" The tyranny of Reformation and Renaissance had dogmatizied the scriptures whose sanction still remained unchallengeable, though many of them had already outlived their utility.

It is true that the Scripture has its useful place in society in as much as it can communicate the divine precepts and commandments to the people and make them obedient to the moral law, but never beyond this periphery of its own. But, in the 17th century, it had encroached upon the realm of metaphysics and had strangled all

---

66. *In Defence of Idealism.*

inquiry into the essence of God. God was supposed to have delivered Himself to the world through the Scripture, through the mouths of the blessed few, through oracles and apocalypse. It is upto man to submit to Him without any question. He, who hesitated, was a heretic, only to be cursed by Divine Dispensation.

This scriptural opium was a stumbling block to all sorts of metaphysical inquiry. Any trace of independent inquiry was borne down as a sin against God, the heavenly Father, 'Descartes had felt the strain of these fetters. And Spinoza, at the cost of society and security, challenged the same authenticity even from his early days at school.

Spinoza should never be mistaken as an obstinate iconoclast. His mission was not to become notorious by breaking everything that he came across. He never despised the church as the 'wily and unregenerate instrument of vicious priests'. We never find in him, either Voltaire's passion for mockery or Strauss's passion for demolition. During his days at The Hague he never missed the sermons if he knew that they were from a sincere and devoted person. What Spinoza wanted was an unchecked scope for growth in all spheres of life. Metaphysics has its place as religion also has its. Neither should extend itself into the domain of the other and arrest its growth. Spinoza was, therefore, only opposed to the tyranny of the church over the just liberties of men. As Mathew Arnold remarks, "His whole soul was filled with desire of the love and knowledge of God and of that only."[67] The faculty of understanding, according to him, was a man's 'eternal part' and he could not brook any impediment that stood in the way of all free development.

As a sensible thinker, he could not do away with the utility of the church. It was the business of the church to inculcate obedience in the masses, but in so doing, never to dictate truth to philosophers. The larger multitude did not pain its head on ultimate problems. It was quite proper, therefore, if he simply believed in the moral sanctions and lived by them without any speculative wisdom. The Scripture and its laws with divine sanctions were of much service to the common man in his ordinary walks of life. Ordinary life was only for living, hence its demands could be satisfied by the given data of morals. But

67. cf. His essay captioned 'Spinoza and the Bible'.

this could not be extended to where the quest after truth came to question. A philosopher could never accept things as given. His search would begin with a recurring 'why' and could only be satisfied when he had conclusive proofs at his disposal. Thus the Scripture, through showing the path of charity and devotion to the multitude, must clear the way for philosophers. Spinoza writes to Blyenburgh, "I say that scripture, since it especially suits and serves the common mass, speaks throughout after human fashion, for the common mass is incapable of understanding exalted things. Philosophers and all who are above the laws, that is to say, those who follow virtue not as embodied in Laws, but from love because it is the best thing, should not stumble over its words."

Spinoza's age was rife with belief in ghosts and miracles. Even the most learned men were its voluntary victims. We know this from the many letters that were coming to Spinoza. In one place, he humorously remarks that if the devil is as God—forsaken, as he is commonly believed to be, he must be so wretched that we ought to pray for him.[68]

Tractatus Theologico-Politicus was anonymously published in 1670. It was a protest, first of its kind, against any acquiescent obedience to the Scriptures and gave a 'new interpretation' to it. Spinoza wrote, "[..] the method of interpreting the Scripture does not widely differ from the method of interpreting Nature—in fact, it is almost the same." The Scripture only bore the opinions of the historians who had recorded them. And to know the real meaning of it, we must also be acquainted with the spirit of the time in which each book was written and to what nation it was addressed. He flatly refused to believe in it if it did not satisfy his reason. "As the scripture," wrote he, "when it was first published, was fitted to the established opinions and to the capacity of the people, so everybody is free to expound it according to his knowledge, and make it agree with his own opinions." Thus we see that Spinoza's approach to the Books was philosophical and historical. He anticipated Mathew Arnold when he treated them not as dogma but as literature. This approach was new of its kind and so brought about a storm in the current theology.

---

68. Short Treatise, Book II, Ch. XXV, p. 143.

The sacred books of Judaism and Christianity were full of particular revelations and glorified them. According to Spinoza, the scope of these devices was to assure men that there was a way of salvation through obedience. This obedience did not wait for any philosophic clarification of the moral sanction but grew in the exercise of justice and charity. Men were content in believing in "a Supreme Being loving justice and charity, whom all men are bound to obey that they may be saved and to worship by showing justice and charity to their neighbours."[69] "Whether He be fire, spirit, light, thought or otherwise, is of no account of faith; nor yet in what manner he is, the type of the right life, [..] to faith it is all one what every man holds touching these things. So again it is indifferent to faith whether one believes that God is everywhere essentially or potentially; that he governs nature freely or by the necessity of His own nature; that he dictates law as a prince, or shows them as eternal truths, that men obey God from absolute free will or by necessity of the divine ordinance, that the reward of good and punishment of wicked men is natural or supernatural." This way of faith, though it cannot be discovered by natural reason, can yet be embraced by people. Thus Spinoza gave simple *Bhakti* its proper place and though admitting its efficacy, kept it away from intruding upon reason.

Philosophically viewed, the scriptures fall short of truth and profess beliefs which cannot be digested by reason. Jehovah, the God of the Jews, was a personal God. Jesus had also been deified by the Christians. Spinoza could not accept this anthropomorphism of the Scriptures as truth. His point was that man had made God in his own image. He wrote, "A triangle, if only it had the power of speech, would say in like manner that God is eminently triangular, and a circle would say that the Divine Nature is eminently circular, and in this way each thing would ascribe its own attributes to God and make itself like into God, while all else would appear to be deformed.[70] This takes us back to Xenophanes, the Greek philosopher who wrote, "if oxen and horses and lions had hands and could paint with their hands, and produce works of art as men do, horses would paint the forms of gods like horses and oxen like oxen. [..] The Ethiopians

69. Tr.Th.Pol.Ch. 14:24.
70. Letter no. 56.

make their Gods black and scrub-nosed, the Thracians say theirs have blue eyes and red hair."[71] Modern philosophy also rejects the idea of personalizing God. It is not the bodily constitution but the spirit of god that has appealed to the wise men of all times. Mahatma Gandhi writes, "God is not a person; Rama, Krishna etc. are called incarnations of God because we attribute divine qualities to them. In truth, they are creations of man's imagination."[72]

God is the essence, the underlying presence pervading the world. It is neither visible to the eyes, nor audible to the ears. Man can feel it but can never perceive it through the senses. As Wordsworth writes, He is a "presence that disturbs me with the joy of elevated thoughts." As Patrick expresses it, "God is the soul of the world, an indwelling spiritual presence, a creative, organizing and perfecting power, the source of our moral, religious and aesthetic ideals."[73] Spinoza sounds quite modern when he says, "To your question whether I have as clear an idea of God as I have of a triangle, I answer in the affirmative. But if you ask me whether I have as clear a mental image of God as I have of a triangle, I shall answer 'no'. For we can not imagine God, but we can, indeed conceive Him."[74]

Plato had conceived a world of ideas above this world of appearances. Aristotle also could not totally escape from this dualism of the real and the unreal. As Bergson stated in a later date, we are all born Platonists. We always conceive an ideal existence towards which all mundane existence is heading. In our ordinary activities of life, we live in terms of ends and purposes, prescribe reward and punishment in virtue and vice. The same idea also we have projected as regards God whom we suppose to be in heaven; ever alert to take account of our deeds and misdeeds. God is a judge; the Christian scripture has also an idea of the Doomsday, when we are summoned before God for a trial. But Plato himself did never apprehend such anthropomorphic development of his conception of ideas. He rebuked with scorn, the religious teachers who described the righteous dead "as reclining on couches at a banquet of the pious, and with garlands

71. J. Burnet, Early Greek philosophy, p. 119.
72. Harijan, 22.6.47.
73. Introduction to Philosophy, p. 394.
74. Letter no. 56.

on their heads spending all eternity in wine bibbing, the fullest reward of virtue in their estimation of everlasting carousal."[75] With the same indignant note, Spinoza turns upon "those who expect to be decorated by God with high rewards for their virtue and their best actions, as for having endured the direct slavery—as if virtue and the service of God were not in itself happiness and perfect freedom."[76] This practice of piety in the hope of virtue or from the fear of dreadful punishments after death, Spinoza cancels away from his conception of moral life in the fifth part of the *Ethic*. (41. Schol)

God is not a person, neither is He the Book-keeping Bureau in the heights of heaven, keeping account of human falls and foibles. He is here upon this earth. Lucretius had imagined Him as looking down from His high heavenly pedestal and taking delight in the sins of imperfect mortals. Spinoza brought Him down to earth. He is not above it, He is it. He is the eternal order of the essence and existence of things. God has no free will, he requires nothing of this sort. He is no whimsical force eager to show Himself away. He acts from His own necessity; He is self determined and is therefore free. He has no choice, nor any moral end. As we have seen before, Spinoza rejects 'finality'. "All the prejudices, which I here mean to lay bare, depend on this point only; to wit, that men commonly suppose all things in Nature to act as themselves do for a purpose; in so much that they make sure that God himself orders all things for some fixed end."[77]

We degrade God if we attribute to Him the doctrine of finality. It is inconsistent with His perfection, "for, if God acts for a designed end, it must needs be that He desireth something which he hath not." Only by our ignorance we make Him limited by bringing in finality.

It should not evade our attention when Spinoza writes, "In no way do I subject God to fate, but I conceive that everything follows with inevitable necessity from the nature of God." He is free but necessary. From the universal point of view, perfection is fullness of being and has nothing to do with the perfection that is relative to man's use or convenience. Thus examining Spinoza's criticism of the contemporary theology, we know that his God is free but not

75. Republic: p. 363.
76. Ethic. II. 49 Schol.
77. Ethic I. Appendix.

exercising choice. He has no design, is not moral in the sense of having preferences.

What does Spinoza say of Jesus Christ? He looked on him as a man of transcendent and unique moral genius. "I believe not that any man ever came to that singular height of perfection but Christ. [..] The wisdom of God, i.e. a wisdom above man's, took man's nature in Christ and that Christ is the way of salvation. But of those things which sundry churches determine concerning Christ, I have naught to say, neither do I deny them, for I am free to confess I comprehend them not." In his letter to Oldenberg in 1675, Spinoza wrote, "I say it is by no means necessary to salvation to know Christ after the flesh; but of the eternal son of God, that is, the eternal wisdom of God, which has shown itself forth in all things, and chiefly in the mind of man, and most chiefly of all in Jesus Christ, we are to think for otherwise. For without this, no one can attain the state of blessedness, since this alone teaches what is true and false, good and evil." In another letter says he of miracle and mystery as no foundations of true religion. "God has no right or left hand, nor is naturally in any one place, but everywhere; the same, and God can not display Himself outside the world in the imaginary space men feign. [..] Christ was gifted with eternity and rose from the dead (the dead in that sense, in which Christ said, 'let the dead bury their dead'), in that by his life and death he gave a singular example of holiness, and he raises his disciples from the dead in so much as they follow this example of his life and death."

Spinoza revolted against all silly superstitions and based religion on reason, justice and piety. By separating metaphysics from theology, he let both scientific inquiry and philosophic speculation breathe freely. Before him, men took to religion from a sense of fear and insignificance. It was congenial to the hegemony of the priests who were secure as long as people feared religion. Spinoza approached religion with the spirit of love of knowledge and clearly demonstrated that the spirit of God was nothing to be feared but only to be lived in. He understood the true essence of religion and in his religious understanding, there was no room for superstition. Heine says of Spinoza: "His life was a copy of the life of his divine kinsman, Jesus Christ."

(i) On Polity And Politics

Spinoza's political ideas can be found in the two books, *Tractatus Theologico-Politicus* and *Tractatus Politicus*. The first book, as we already know, was published in 1670. The second he left unfinished and it was published as a part of the *Opera Posthuma* in 1677. Both the books raised a gall of irritating excitement in the minds of the people at large who condemned them as the works of an atheist.

The political doctrine of Spinoza has its basis on his ethical doctrine. According to the latter, self-preservation is the duty of every individual and each can best do so only in society. 'Man is a God to man'. When men combine in society, 'This society, firmly established by law and with a power of self-preservation, is called a state and those who are protected by its right, are called citizens."[78]

In the *Tr. Th. Pol.*, Spinoza comes very near to Rousseau's 'Social Contract' theory. He speculates the formation of society from a previous state of 'natural' anarchy. "When we reflect that men without mutual help, or the aid of reason, must live most miserably [..], we shall plainly see that men must necessarily come to an agreement to live together as securely and well as possible if they are to enjoy, as a whole, the rights which naturally belong to them as individuals, and their life should be no more conditioned by the force and desire of individuals, but by the power and the will of the whole body."[79] "Men are united by their need of one another." "Men would, without mutual help, necessarily spend their lives in utmost wretchedness and without the development of reason."[80] If human nature had been so fashioned that men most desired that which is for their welfare, no devices would be required for making men live in harmony and trust; but as it is evident that human nature has been constituted in a very different way, the state should necessarily be arranged that all, rulers as well as ruled, may, *nolens volens*, do what the common welfare demands."[81]

---

78. Ethic: IV. 37 Schol. 2.
79. Philosophy of Spinoza, p. 300.
80. Tr.Th.Pol: ch. 16.
81. *Ibid*: Ch. 6.

But in *Tractatus Politicus*, a product of a more matured brain, Spinoza gives an account of the origin of society in a purely naturalistic fashion. Here he anticipates the most modern of all the theories of state so far expounded. As a radical empiricist, he proclaims that "human beings are so oraganised that they can not live outside the pale of society."[82] "Men, be they savage or civilized, are everywhere found united and forming civil societies."[83] By nature, man is both an individualist and a member of a community. Society does not destroy our egoism, nor our egoism withholds us from participating in the common life. After a careful analysis of the 'contract' theory, we come to this logical conclusion that the conception of 'natural right' is a misnomer without preconceiving any society. Right and duty can come only after society.

As we have previously seen, Spinoza's approach is that of love and sympathy. In his politics also, the same spirit prevails; he theorizes on society not as a sermonizer, nor as one who is eager to break men into one's henchmanship. He writes: "[..] politicians have the reputation of being much more concerned to set traps for their fellowmen than to watch over their interests; and their main title of honour is not wisdom but cunning. They have learnt at the school of facts that there will be vices as long as there will be men." He praised the politicians as saying nothing, which is too far removed from reality.[84]

If all men in society would be guided only by the dictates of reason, the individual will of self-preservation would peacefully reconcile itself with the preservation of society. But taking the world as it is, we see that the reason of man has been atrophied by endless affects and emotions and infrequently our interests fall one upon another. Thus the need of a state authority is proved in so far as we can live in mental adjustment. The state will minister to the peace in society and let everyone preserve his own self as long as he is not an obstacle to another.

Politics is not ethics. The latter deals with men as they should be, but politics with men as they actually are. The rule of politics cannot

---

82. Tr. Pol.: I. 3.
83. *Ibid* I. 7.
84. *Ibid* I. 2.

be deferred because men have not become strong ethically. Rather politics can be more sensibly used as a means to attain ethical perfection. The state, side by side with maintaining order in society, can lead men to moral excellence by its code of discipline. Therefore the best policy for a government will be that of expediency, that is, of following the best of all the alternative situations present. "Freedom and strength of mind are virtues in private men, but the virtue of government is safety." What is esteemed good or bad for the society, becomes right or wrong for its men. Modern English philosophers have called it 'positive morality'. What the state prescribes as duty or justice is duty and justice for its citizens. Because, Spinoza affirms, only the state is empowered to determine law in view of the interests of the citizens. Those who disobey and tamper with public safety should be taken to task. Crimes are to be met with by condign punishment.

Spinoza's state smacks of the Great Leviathian of Hobbes, who is supposed to be his political hierophant. Many have charged Spinoza with preaching absolutism. Melamed remarks that the state of Spinoza is a 'tamed beast', a 'mechanism' where the people are there only to obey the laws of the state. He accuses Spinoza's philosophy as mechanistic, subjecting human beings to inviolable laws of nature and perorates that Spinoza's state was the consistent outcome of his theory of the universe. But these accusations may be due to the fact that as the world has long been a victim of authority, it has a tendency to shudder always at all authority. Spinoza, in fact, never wanted to install, in his state, an absolute prince of the Machiavellian pattern. From his very inception as a philosopher, he was all along a lover and vindicator of freedom. All his works speak aloud of his spirit of individual freedom. Many passages can be taken from the *Tr.Th.Pol.* to demonstrate him where he actually stands. "It makes for slavery; not peace, to deliver all power to one man." "It is better that just counsels of a realm should be laid open to enemy, than that the wicked secrets should be concealed from citizens." There are, surely, limits to the state's exercising its authority over the populace. Because like every individual, it is incumbent upon the state that it also should be guided by reason. It can only be obeyed without question as long as it promotes social solidarity and health. "If I say that I may of right do so as I will with this table, I suppose not thereby that I have a right to make the table eat grass." Thus the state can not be justified in compelling its citizens to absolute submission, contrary to human nature. In case of an excess like this, the state may be superseded by the people who may take recourse to revolutions.

Spinoza speaks of various forms of governments. Monarchy is the rule by one man and subsists best by the advice of counsellors. In aristocracy, the sovereign power belongs to selected citizens. Spinoza also visualizes a polity, consisting of a number of confederated cities of equal power. Democracy is the governance by representatives [..]" If each individual hands over the whole of his power to the body politic, the latter will then possess sovereign natural right over all things; that is, it will have sole and unquestioned dominion, and everyone will be bound to obey under pain of the severest punishment. A body politic of this kind is called a Democracy, which may be defined as a society which welds its power as a whole."[85] This democracy, rather a peculiar one of its kind, is based on a franchise fixed by law. As Pollock warns us, we should not take franchise in its modern sense, but it is simply the right to take part, in some way or other, in the government, which, however, includes voting. Voting qualifications may be there in respect of age, primogeniture and on the payment of taxes of a certain amount. Aliens, women, infants, serfs and criminals are disenfranchised. Of women, Spinoza writes, "It may be asked whether women are under men's authority by nature or by convention. If we consult experience, we shall find the cause to be their weakness. [..] If by nature, women are equal to men, surely among nations, so many and so different, some would be found where both sexes rule alike and others where men are ruled by women. And since this is not the case, one may assert that women have not, by nature, equal right with men." If Spinoza comes down again to our world, he will be disillusioned to find his dictum refuted. The age, then, was rife with the 'master theory' of men and Spinoza only echoed the same. It would be interesting to know whether Spinoza qualified women for his life of reason and the intellectual love of God.

Spinoza gives the upper hand to democracy. "I believe it to be of all forms of government the most natural, and the most consonant with individual liberty. In it no one transfers his natural right so

---

85. Philosophy of Spinoza, p. 304.

absolutely that he has no further voice in affairs; he only hands it over to the majority of a society, whereof he is a unit. Thus all men remain, as they were in the state of nature, equals."[86]

The object of a commonwealth is peace and protection; its excellence consists in men living in amity and obeying the law. "The general end of the state is peace and security of life."[87] And to maintain peace, the state wants that everyone should abide by law. But the laws, in order to be worth the name, must be based on reason and should not be arbitrary and blind. "That state is the freest, where laws are founded on sound reason, so that every member of it may, if he will, be free; that is, live with full consent under the entire guidance of reason."

The citizen does not become a slave simply because he obeys the laws of the state. Ideally conceived, the laws of the state and the private sanctions of the individual man living a life of reason do never collide. As Spinoza writes, "The true slave is he who is led away by his pleasures and can neither see what is good for him nor act accordingly. He alone is free who lives with free consent under the entire guidance of reason."[88] In a state where the weal of the whole people, not that of those only who rule, is the supreme purpose of the law, obedience to the sovereign power does not make man a slave but a subject.

But yet the state should not emphasize upon conducting men by law only. Its excellence is in leading men to voluntary obedience than in compelling them. "He who seeks to regulate everything by law is more likely to arouse vices than to reform them."[89] The aim of state is always a positive one, it is not to make itself felt only negatively, that is, by restrictive promulgations. Spinoza writes, "The end of the state is to deliver each man from fear, so that he may be able to live with the utmost possible security. The end is not to make rational beings into brute beasts or into automata. It is to lead men to live by and exercise a free reason, that they may not waste their strength in hatred, anger and guile, nor act unfairly towards one another. Thus the

---

86. *Ibid*, p. 306.
87. Tr. Pol. V2.
88. Philosophy of Spinoza, p. 305.
89. Philosophy of Spinoza, p. 338.

end of state is really liberty or freedom."[90] Again, " A government which aims at nothing else but to guide men by fear will be rather free from defects than possessed of merit. Men are to be so guided that they may deem themselves not to be guided but to live after their own mind and of their own free resolve, and that they be kept to allegiance by love of freedom."

In another pamphlet, *Tractatus Bellico Pacificus*, Spinoza maintains that human nature being what it is, peace can only be maintained by force. But this is not the desirable way open to it. As he writes in *Tr.Pol.*, "If slavery, rudeness and desolation are to be called peace, then is peace the most wretched state of mankind. Truly there are more and sharper disputes between parents and children than between masters and slaves, and yet it were no good house-keeping to make the father into a master, and hold the children for slaves." By peace Spinoza never meant the peace of the iron rule or the peace of the grave. "A commonwealth whose subjects do not rise in arms because they are overcome by terror is rather to be spoken of as being without war than as enjoying peace. For peace is not mere absence of war, but an excellence proceeding from high-mindedness; since obedience is the constant will to execute, what, by the general decree of the commonwealth, to be done. Moreover, a commonwealth whose peace depends upon the sluggishness of its subjects that are led about like sheep to learn but slavery, may more properly be called a wilderness than a commonwealth. When, therefore, we call that government best, under which men live in peace. To understand that life of man which consistent not only in the circulation of blood and the other properties common to all animals, but whose chief part is reason and the true life and excellence of the mind."[91] Even in the twentieth century, there are instances of a state being formed by men, having only that animal unity of blood. But to Spinoza, it was the human virtues that brought men together.

Spinoza's state denounces all ecclesiastical pretensions and reject all claims, on grounds of religion or otherwise, to set up a jurisdiction, equal or superior to that of the civil power. It should not extend its patronage to any particular religious institution. Religion is man's

90. Tr.Th.Pol.Ch. 20.
91. Tr.Pol.Ch. 5.

personal thing. It can never be collectivized without fermenting jeopardy. Even the churches, Spinoza makes the point very clear, shall be built at the cost of the worshippers. But supporting no religion, the state should not, also on the other hand, arrest religious toleration and freedom of thought.

The citizens are to be led to reason by education. Self-education can raise us from the dross we live in. Spinoza always distinguished education from instruction. The latter is a routine process of one's giving and others' taking. Education is always mutual. It is only by developing man's own potentialities that he can be educated. Spinoza writes, "Governments should never found academies, for they serve more to oppress than to encourage genius. The unique method of making the arts and sciences flourish is to allow every individual to teach what he thinks, at his own risk and peril."[92] The spirit can also be traced from Spinoza's own life, his association with Van den Ende and his own circle of pupils at The Hague.

Spinoza championed the cause of free thought. He suffered many perils to maintain his freedom of mind. One of the reasons of writing the Tr.Th.Pol. was also "the freedom of philosophizing and of saying what we think; this I desire to indicate in every way, for here it is always suppressed through the excessive authority and impudence of the preachers." [93] In his political treatise he profusely pleaded for this freedom arguing that it would never imperil the smooth running of the state. "It follows from the words of scripture," he wrote, "that they are anti-Christs, who persecute the opinions of the just men who differ from them in opinion and do not maintain their doctrines. They, that love justice and charity are thereby only found to be believers and whoever persecutes believers is anti-Christ." "What greater misfortune for a state can be conceived than that honorable men should be sent like criminals into exile, because they hold diverse opinions which they can not disguise."[94] In the preface to the same book, he says, "If acts only could be made the ground of criminal persecutions and words were always to pass free, sedition would be divested of every semblance of justification." Again, "Schisms

92. Tractatus Politicus. Ch. 8-49.
93. Letter no. 30.
94. Tractatus Theologico-Politicus, Ch. 40.

proceed, not from the study of truth, that foundation of meekness and moderation, but from an auspicious humour of prescribing to others, and therefore, they are to be accounted schismatics who damn other men's writings and stir up the waspish multitude against them, for they are truly disturbers of public peace, who, in a free commonwealth, would take away the liberty of men's judgement, which ought not to be suppressed."

From these exhaustive quotations, it can be well imagined what a strain a philosopher or a free thinker had to undergo in the society Spinoza was brought up in. With that background of strain and censure, if we read into the spirit of Spinoza's political doctrines, we can rightly know the density of the fury that rose against him from high circles of state and religion.

For various reasons, Spinoza has been cast into shade by Hobbes, his contemporary in politics. But we can conclude with Pollock, "The judgement of history is not always the judgement of philosophy. Spinoza's doctrine rests on a wider and more generous view of human life, it is less encumbered with fictions, it aims at a higher mark. It is the work, not of a powerful mind which has expoused the cause of a party and makes philosophy a partisan, but of a philosopher who is proud of being a citizen."[95]

Spinoza, let us recall the incident at The Hague when the riotous crowd had come to break into his room, had thus defined himself before his landlord, "I am a good Republican."

---

95. Pollock's book, p. 338.

3

Spinoza Through the Ages

Men fear thought as they fear nothing on earth, more than ruin, more even than death. Thought is subversive and revolutionary, destructive and terrible, thought is merciless to privilege, established institutions and comfortable habits, thought is anarchic and lawless, indifferent to authority, careless of the well-tried wisdom of the ages. Thought looks into the pit of hell and is not afraid.

—Bertrand Russell

The West has the ill repute of denouncing its great men if they do not fit in with its traditional fads and fashions. Instances are redundant in history which speak of free thinkers having been condemned to black inquisition, patriots outlawed and saviours burnt as evil spirits. It has never been tired of shooting and subduing those who came too early to its society. Spinoza was too early, he was but a Crypto-Jew in the Christian Republic. So he had to pay in full, the penality for thinking like an independent and wise man.

During his lifetime very few people did recognize his worth. His society was much limited to his circle of friends, who took regular lessons from him. Silent and single in his country—life of contemplation, his life was a challenge to all contemporary scholars in philosophy and science who looked upon this taciturn Jew with jealous curiosity. Spinoza's glory was not woven by the wreaths of royal cheers as Leibnitz's was, neither was he a learned and recognized professor in any university. Spinoza was a peculiar specimen entirely unfitting to the age. He was so silent and satisfied in normal life, and yet so revolting in mind. The society had been used to give its laurels only to those wiseacres who could easily come to the limelight. Spinoza always loved to grow in a philosophical calm and hence was naturally condemned before he was rightly known.

Among his circle of friends and correspondents were many great men of science and philosophy. It included Boyle and Oldenburg from England and Leibnitz and De Witt from the continent. Spinoza wrote regularly to 'the honorable' Boyle who did never send a direct reply, except through Oldenburg, to this 'odd' philosopher of Amsterdam. Leibnitz came in contact with Spinoza through the latter's' interest in optics. Though Boyle never wrote directly to Spinoza, his 'Boyle letters' was partly his reactions to Spinoza's *Tractatus Theologico-Politicus*, and was meant to prove the truth of Christianity against 'notorious infidels viz, atheists, theists, pagans, Jews and Mohammedans.' Leibnitz, the dual personality, who was spiritually a cringing flunkey of the German court, once paid a visit to Spinoza. Perhaps he had totally sidetracked the latter's philosophical worth when he remarked that Spinoza's book on theology was 'an unbearably free thinking book.' And after visiting Spinoza and going through his books, he said, "He has a strange metaphysic, full of paradoxes."

Both the *Theologico-Politicus* and the *Opera Posthuma* were condemned by the authorities as preaching atheism. The earlier was confined to Spinoza's views on theology. From the dawn of history, man had been thinking on theological terms. Religion was the only inexhaustible store-house of all his knowledge and theology, the giver of all wisdom. It was Spinoza who changed the entire table of popular notion and divorced theology from intruding upon science and philosophy. He called for a historiographical analysis of the scripture and testing its content by the criterion of reason alone. Is he not speaking the very profanation of sacred religion?—the wise men of the time began to question themselves. The people were alarmed with the dread of sacrilege, and books and pamphlets poured in refutation of Spinoza's *Theologico-Politicus*. 'Blasphemous, atheistic, deceitful, soul-destroying works of Spinoza'—such were the epithets the defenders of faith piled upon him! One critic wrote of him as one of the 'three most cursed villains that ever walked this earth.' One German pamphleteer, Hax Grunwald wrote in 1702, 'Especially Spinoza seems to have been hired by Satan to develop atheism'. Some of the early German critics called him, 'son of hell', 'dog' and 'skum'. After Spinoza died, a section of the people expressed their sincere spite by regularly spitting on the grave of this inveterate heretic.

Spitzelius criticized *Spinoza's Theologico-Politicus* in the following words, "That impious author blinded by a prodigious presumption, was so impudent and so full of impiety, as to maintain that prophecies were only grounded upon the fancy of the prophets; and that the prophets and the apostles wrote naturally according to their own light and knowledge, without any revelation or order from God; that they accommodated religion, as well as they could, to the genius of those who lived at that time and established it upon such principles as were then well known and commonly received."[1]

The first biography of Spinoza was published in 1705 in the Dutch language by Colerus, the German Minister of the Lutheran Congregation at The Hague. After giving many interesting details of Spinoza's personality and daily life, he has thus drawn out his remark on the *Tr.Th.Pol.*: "If what Spinoza affirms were true, one might indeed very well say that the Bible is a wax-nose, which may be turned and shaped at one's will, a glass through which anybody may exactly see what pleases his fancy; a fool's cap, which may be turned and fitted at one's pleasure a hundred several ways. The Lord confound thee, Satan, and stop thy mouth!" Blyenbergh, one of Spinoza's correspondents also remarked on the above book that "The author endeavours to overthrow the Christian religion and baffle all our hopes, which are grounded upon it."

We gave this long stretch of interesting criticisms only to indicate how revolutionary a book was Spinoza's and how it reacted on the stale and stagnant beliefs of the day. No one gave him a serious reading, nevertheless, the stir he gave to theology brought him vile vituperations.

So also the *Opera Posthuma*. The whole world, as it were, cursed the satanic spirit that was gone! The Dutch Government suppressed the book as "profane, atheistical and blasphemous, seducing the innocent reader from the true way of salvation."

A manifestation of Spinozism rose within a generation of Spinoza's death in the reformed church of the Netherlands, with Van

---

1. Infelix Literator, p. 363.

Hattem as the leader. But Hattemism was mainly imbued with the mystical ideas of Spinoza and blatantly exaggerated it. Yet they did enough to draw the authorities' eyes of suspicion and a number of their pamphlets was consigned to fire by the Government as being 'full of abominable and blasphemous sentiments of the Libertines, modern Spinozists, Hattemists and free thinkers'. Another victim was Leenhof for bringing out a book *Heaven on Earth* (1703) attempting to construct a rationalized system of Christian ethics embodying most of the doctrines of Spinoza.

Spinoza was forgotten till after a century of his death. His books were never read by any philosopher. The reason was the enmity he had created with the orthodox theologians by his new criticism of the Bible. The Cartesians disbelieved him for his independent spirit; many of them disowned him from fear of being suspected as his associates. Leibnitz, though recognizing Spinoza's worth as an optician, denounced his philosophy and told that he did nothing but cultivate some of the seeds sown by Descartes. "Spinoza begins, where Descartes ends, in naturalism." As a French writer has uttered in a like tone, 'Let us forgive Descartes for having raised up Spinoza."

Meanwhile, the philosophers all through the ages have only passed stray remarks on Spinoza. Corresponding to the latter's time; it was the age of dogmatic empiricism in England. The English philosophers-- Locke, Berkeley and Hume-- started with actuality. Their method was inductive; their philosophy was generalizing from the data of perception. Hence Spinoza, 'who began with God, could have little headway in England. The above three philosophers only made passing remarks on Spinoza. Locke defines him with Hobbes as 'those justly decried authors, Berkeley speaks of his work as 'wild imagination' and one of "modern theisms". Hume betrays his lamentable ignorance of Spinoza calling him a "famous atheist," and his fundamental principles 'a hideous hypothesis'.[2] Clarke described him as 'the most celebrated patron of atheism of his time', and exposed his 'variety, folly and weakness'.

Spinoza was also coldly received in France. Condillac, in his *Traité des systèmes* accuses Spinoza of writing from an anti-

---

2. Treatise of Human Nature, 4/5.

metaphysical point of view and under the geometrical fallacy. He treats him as a dogmatic trifler who deceives himself with an unintelligible scholastic jargon. His definitions are loose, his axioms far from being true, his propositions fantastic and barren. Voltaire speaks highly of Spinoza's personal life but denounces his doctrines as impious. Montesquieu was accused of Spinozism for having ventured to treat historical and political problems in a scientific manner. Rousseau, as can be inferred from his 'Nature' theory, must have read Spinoza and found interest in him. Summing up, we see, Spinoza's name—had become a catchword for anti theological polemics and no one cared to see what the philosopher had actually said.

But from 1780, a new phase began in the interpretation of Spinoza and it can be rightly called the revival of Spinozism. It look shape in the reaction to the Biblicism of Reformation in Germany. People, now tired of the apothesis of the latter, found a sympathetic vein in Spinoza's scientific spirit. If a date can be fixed for this new phase, Pollock says, it must be Lessing's conversation with Jacobi in 1780. Though nothing like a school of Neo-Spinozism was created, the thinkers began to consider Spinoza's ideas as having much philosophical worth that could not be by-passed in the name of atheism.

Lessing had very carefully studied Spinoza. In the historic conversation, he says to Jacobi, "To grasp Spinoza requires a mental effort too long and too stubborn for them (people). And no one has grasped him to whom a single line in the *Ethic* has remained obscure." As Merz remarks, "Lessing and many of his followers certainly found, in the philosophy of Spinoza, a resting place and refuge from the prosaic moralizing and shallow rationalism of the Deists in England and the Encyclopaedists in France. Compared with these, Spinoza rose before them as an inspired writer, as one who looked at the great life problems not from a utilitarian and narrowly moralizing point of view, but *sub specie aeternitatis*."[3]

Within a decade's time after the death of Lessing, Spinoza dominated the whole of the German society. Herder, the German

3. Merz, History of European Thought in the 19th Century, Vol. III. p. 123.

philosopher, believed that Spinozism would become not the religion, but the philosophy of the future, in which all philosophical systems will be united. The light of Spinoza shone large even in spite of the rise of Kant. Kant could never cast him into shade. On the contrary, Spinoza's appeal to the new minds was so great that Kant had to take a careful and definite stand, since it became clear to him that many of his disciples were deserting him in favour of Spinoza. Hemans writes in his *Kant-Studien* that "in his whole life Kant had a resentment against Spinoza." Spinoza remained ever a riddle for him in spite of his mathematical method. Constantine Bruner has expressed the opinion that everyone must be either a Spinozist or a Kantian. Comparing the two, Melamed writes, "The modern intellectual world is overwhelmingly Spinozistic. Kant created only a school of thought, but Spinoza gave birth to a new culture and religion. Kant was interested in recognition, Spinoza in salvation. Everyone is interested in Spinoza but only philosophers are concerned with Kant."

Spinoza received a much-esteemed recognition from the successors of Kant. Though Fichte differs much from Spinoza both in his method and conclusions, he had nevertheless studied him and felt his power. In his works, he also gives a summary criticism of Spinoza's Substance. After Fichte came Hegel and Schelling. Hegel found in Spinoza what he missed in Kant, namely, a more ultimate connection between knowledge and action and theory and practice. According to him, Spinoza was the ground of all philosophy. "To be a philosopher," he wrote, "you must be a Spinozist." Hegel's *Phenomenology of Mind* may be taken as "a logical development of the main idea which was most clearly expressed in advance by Spinoza when he identified the order which prevails in things with the order which prevails in our thoughts about things."[4]

Schopenhauer, the prince among the pessimists, sensed only optimism in Spinoza. "Pantheism is essentially and necessarily optimism," he wrote, "Spinoza's *Substantia aeterna*, the inner character of the world, which he entitles Deus, is according to its character and value, the Jehovah, the God-Creator. To Spinoza, the world and everything in it, is excellent and as it should be. In short Spinozism is optimism pure and simple." He remarked, in

4. Merz, p. 371.

concluding, that Spinoza's spiritual homeland was on the banks of holy Ganges.

Nietzsche was an out and out Spinoza enthusiast. His praises for the latter take the form of exclamations. Thus he writes in *Thus Spake Zarathustra*, "I am full of delight, I have a predecessor, and what a predecessor! I almost did not know Spinoza! That I have an urge for him was a turn of the instinct. The most abnormal and lonely thinker is nearest to me in just these things; he denies the freedom of will,—the ends—the moral world order, the unegoistic, the evil. My solitude is now at least a dualitude!"

Spinoza remained prominent even till the twentieth century. Hartmann, though a follower of Leibnitz, defended the monism of Spinoza. In England, he was taken up by Herbert Spencer. Waundt and Lotze in Germany, Bergson and Renouvier in France were much influenced by him. Count Keyserling characterizes him as one of the Masters of Ageless Wisdom.

Most of the scholars are unanimous in denying all aesthetic sense in Spinoza. Pollock says that he had no taste for poetry. Sorely asserts that he hardly had reflected at all on the beauty aspect of life. But it is rather surprising to see him rediscovered by the poets of almost all countries of Europe. Perhaps, as James Arther remarks, "There is something in the quality of Spinoza's thought which strikes deeper into the source of beauty, than recognized conventional standards of aesthetics."[5] Spinozism, as a theme in literature, wrought a miracle in the existing classical age of formality, cold logic and artificiality. Spinoza's God or Nature pervaded the entire universe of things. The 18th century poets were enchanted when they saw in him that all things vibrated with God's spirit. 'God is in me and I am in God' swept the age of poetic thought to the new age of romantic revival. Therefore, it is not strange that Spinoza was recognized and followed in literature even prior to philosophy. He was full of poetry and devotion to the new minds. He bridged the rift which had long separated the scope of poetry from that of philosophy. Poetry reappeared in the Greek role of *Hen Kai Pan*. Before Spinoza, nature poetry was but a part-by-part narration of phenomena, a soulless enunciation. Spinoza gave it a unity, rather a unifying vision and

---

5. Spinozian Wisdom, p. XIX.

divined our world of perception. The new movement started in Germany with Goethe, Lessing and Schiller.

Goethe writes that after many years of restless queries, he found solace in Spinoza. "I turned for relief to my old asylum, to Spinoza, in whose ethic, I found daily entertainment for several weeks, and as since the date of my last acquaintance with him, my culture had been deepened and purified, I now found to my admiration a great deal in him new and unexpected, exercising on me an influence fresh and all its own."[6] But what especially riveted me to him was the boundless disinterestedness, which shone forth in every sentence. That wonderful sentiment, 'He who truly loves God must not require God to love him in return' filled my mind."[7] Lewes remarks that Spinoza was to Goethe what Kant was to Schiller. Spinoza, Goethe says, was never an atheist. He was the most theistical of theists, and the most Christian of Christians. "If I had to name the book that of all I know, agrees best with my view I could only name the 'Ethic'. I hold more and more firmly to worshipping God with this so called atheist." This is how his poems reflect the spirit of Spinoza:

He loves the inner world to move, to view
Nature in Him, Himself in Nature too.

Others, who were influenced greatly by Spinoza, were Schleiermacher, Heine and Novalis. Novalis called Spinoza, the 'God-intoxicated' philosopher.

Hippolyte Taine made Spinoza's influence widespread in France. He brought in naturalism in French literature and was the first to apply the theory of environment in aesthetic evaluations. Victor Hugo thought of God as eternal and indefinable. "Even the attempt to praise him in human words is already blasphemy." He wrote; "The age of the Romantic Revival in English literature owes much to Spinoza. The latter's love of Nature permeated the divine spirit in poetry, and his love of man was the victual of poets who sang the equality of man." Except Keats, all the poets of this school took much from Spinoza's conception of one God in whom everything has its being.

---

6. Goethe: Autobiography and Annals: p. 405.
7. Lewes: Life and words of Goethe: p. 173.

Wordsworth's natural idealism was much shaped by Spinoza's ideas. To Wordsworth, God is the 'eternal wisdom and spirit of the universe that gives to forms and images a breath and everlasting motion.' He is 'all conscious presence of the universe,' writes Coleridge. He regards the *Ethic* as one of the three great works since Christ.[8] Byron discovered the one universe through his observations of it. In a letter, he confessed that he would rather be a Spinozist than a Christian. In his famours '*Child Harold*,[9] Byron wrote,

"I live not in myself, but I become
Portion of that around me"

Shelley was the greatest mystic and visionary in the Neo-Romantic group. He knew life to be "a dome of many-coloured glass that stains the radiance of eternity." He was an eager student of Spinoza's *Theologico-Politicus*. It was, in many ways, of equal nature to his maiden pamphlet, *In Defence of Atheism*. He has inserted a quotation from the just quoted book of Spinoza in his notes to his *Queen Mab*, and there are proofs showing that he had started translating it into English. Byron was to write a life sketch of Spinoza in way of a preface to the translation. But the plan could not materialize owing to Shelley's premature death. Many lines can be quoted from Shelley to show how he was imbued with the idea of Spinoza's one and eternal Substance. In his *Ode to Intellectual Beauty* he sings of the *Causa Sui*:

The awful shadow of some unseen power
Floats though unseen amongst us.

In *Ethic* (III 59 Schol) Spinoza uses the simile of the calm sea for his Substance. A like treatment can be traced in Shelley's *Laon and Cynthia*:

One mind, the type of all the moveless wave
Whose calm reflects all moving things that are,
Necessity, and love, and life, the grave.

---

8. Biographia Literaria, Ch. X.
9. III. 72.

Among others who were influenced by Spinoza were Carlyle, Mathew Arnold and Froude in England and AE. in Ireland. John Tolland was the first poet to compose Spinozistic hymns. His line, 'The world is One and One is the world' hears just like a sentence from Spinoza.

In America, Spinoza's spirit can be found deeply permeated in the new religious movement of the transcendentalists, with their leader in Emerson. Emerson once mentioned that Spinoza was his saint. Thoreau, the solitary aspirant of Lake Walden was also charmed by Spinoza's stainless life and dispassionate thinking. Spinoza's greatest American disciple is surely Walt Whitman, the singer of the soul. From the beginning to the end of his life, he proclaimed the same doctrine of the essential unity of God, Man and Nature.

Spinoza, the mystic, has influenced modern science more than anyone, after Bacon. His defiant call to clear the way for science, his contemplation of the universe as one process run by the one law of Nature were priceless assets for scientific studies. Modern cosmology owes much to Spinoza in this sense. Following his footsteps, Wundt and Haeckel in Germany and Taine in France have made a physiological approach to psychological problems. In fact, Bergson bases his entire treatment of dreams on the ground of physiology. Fechner's psychological researches owe much to Spinoza. Einstein has often asserted his faith in the God of Spinoza. Reichenbach, Plank and many other physicists have been much influenced by his world picture. The God of Spinoza is co-existent with Nature. All discrimination between the spirit and the flesh has been obliterated. In whatever field one endeavours and searches for truth, he is serving the same God Who is One. As Pollock, with full justice to Spinoza, remarks, "Spinoza tends more and more to become the philosopher of the men of science."

From the very prime of his life, Spinoza was a bad recipient of the beliefs and conventions in vogue and as a consequence, his tribe could not give him accommodation in the long run. It had invoked a thousand curses upon the 'atheist' and drove him out from the Synagogue. Spinoza was sworn to his fate with joy and lived always at a distance from the tribe. But today the Jewish spirit is wholly Spinozistic. The three Jewish movements worth noting, the Reform movement in Germany, the Haskalah Movement in Eastern Europe and the Zionist Movement in Central Europe are directly traceable to

Spinoza. The modern Jew is purely secular in outlook and never believes in Judaism as mere sacerdotalism. The old orthodox creed is now found only in the history books. Modern Jewish literature has been much shaped by Spinozism. Spinoza is the leader of the modern Jewish enlightenment. He was the first man in Western Europe to recognize, in Jewry, not merely a religious, but also an ethnic group.

Melamed shows that Bismark, the Great German, was much influenced by Spinoza. In his moments of mental uneasiness, it is reliably alleged, he would always concentrate on Spinoza's *Ethic*. The reading of this book gave him the same refreshing calm as working a geometric problem. Busch, in his biography of Bismark, writes, "Bismark occupied himself with Spinoza in his student days, and though we do not know to what an extent he had adjusted himself to the latter's world-concept, we have a right to assume that it considerably influenced him and that it was one of the causes of his Weltschmerz, which attacked him in those days and which later on, coloured his entire mentality."

In recent days, it is very interesting to remark the growing popularity of Spinoza in Stalin's Russia. In 1927, the Russian Government proclaimed Spinoza as the official philosopher of the state. Deborin, the modern Russian philosopher, gave much value to Spinoza both as a dialectician and as a materialist. Judged from its historical movement and direction, he argued, Spinoza belonged to materialism. The Russian philosophers were ready to go back to Plekhanov's theory that materialism could be characterized as a certain form of Spinozism. But others like Axelrod and Timianski held Spinoza to be an outright idealist. It is calculated that during 1917-38, 55200 copies of books on Spinoza were published in the Soviet Russia.[10]

Spinoza never found a school of his own. Quoting Pollock, 'His aim was not to leave behind him disciples pledged to the letter of his teaching.' But it is rather strange to find him getting recognition from such varied quarters. When he remained inscrutable and neglected, enemies in the schools of thought came together in their enthusiasm to denounce him. And after his personality and philosophy received the first recognition, we also see him welcomed from almost all

10. John Somerville, Soviet Philosophy, p. 218, 236.

stations. The mystic, the moralist, the common man of society and also the scientist all see something in Spinoza which is their own too. Spinoza has been big enough to give room for all schools of thought. Only such a receptacle can satisfy the yearnings of even contradictory elements.

Coming down to the most recent years of research, we often come across the Spinozistic spirit implicit in it. It does, in no way, suggest that Spinoza had already expounded those recent theories in their full import and that they were simply reiterated by the modernists. Knowledge is never a process of sensational findings; it is rather an evolutionary process. No one of its findings do owe its exposition exclusively to its direct exposure. It only advances stride by stride with various thinkers all through the ages. In that sense, Bergson's can be called a descent from the eternal flux of Heraclitus. In the same way, we see in Spinoza, also the faintest suggestions of many of the most recent principles of science that have caused sensation in the modern mind. In the second part of *Ethic*, (18 Schol.) Spinoza writes: "From the thought of the word pomum, a Roman immediately turned to the thought of the fruit, which has no resemblance to the articulate sound pomum, nor anything in common with it, excepting this, that the body of that man was often affected by the thing and the sound; that is to say, he often heard the word pomum when he saw the fruit. [..] And thus each person in turn from one thought to this and that thought, according to the manner in which he has been accustomed to connect and bind together the images of things in his mind." How little the theologically bent mind of the 17th century knew that in these words, Spinoza was anticipating a truth, only found in the 20th century through the experiments of Pavlov. This is known as the theory of Conditioned Reflex arrived at by him in his experiments with the dogs. Next comes the psychology of projection. In the *Ethic* (V 10 Schol.), we read, "Indeed it is certain that those covet glory the most who are loudest in declaiming against its abuse and the variety of the world. [...] So also a man who has not been well received by his mistress thinks of fickleness nothing but the fickleness of women, their faithlessness, and their other off proclaimed failings all of which he forgets as soon as he is taken into favour by his mistress again." And we wretched creatures of this age know it best when we suffer from our own emotions, our own bully. This faculty of projection plays a great part in all of our lives and is due, as Freud interprets it, to 'immediate relation of inner excitations to receptive organs' or 'thrusting painful objects by ego on outer world!'

A triangle, had it the power of forming and expressing ideas, would picture a triangular God. Quoting one of Voltaire's witticisms, 'God created man in his own image and man responded by returning the compliment.' In one of his letters, Spinoza suspected if God would appear triangular to the triangle. In his *Tractus Theologicus-Politicus*, we read him saying that the prophet's ideas about God tell us more about the prophet than about God. He points out (II 16.cor. 2) "that the ideas we have of external bodies indicate the constitution of our own body rather than the nature of external bodies,' and shows, in the scholium to the next proposition how Paul's idea of Peter tells us more about Paul than about Peter. To this, he gives the term, 'images of things.' This tendency of the mind to 'imagine' has also been traced by more than one modern thinker and in more than one branches of study. William James calls it the 'psychologist's fallacy'. John Ruskin gives a whole essay to expound the same idea, which he calls the 'pathetic fallacy.' Santayana detects it as 'normal madness'. In the terminology of Freudian psychoanalysis, it is 'transference.' This so-called phenomenon of transference, Freud says, 'arises spontaneously in all human relations. It has no foundation in any real relation and must be derived from every respect from the old wish-fancies of the patient which have become unconscious.[11] Conscious wish-fancies are not a disease, they are harmful only when unconscious. With a like import, Spinoza says, "The mind is not in error because it imagines, but only in so far as it considers as wanting in an idea which excludes the existence of those things which it imagines as present."[12]

Spinoza's brilliance lies in de-sentimentalizing mental science and pointing out to us to know our affectations of mind by their causes. Nothing is outside his all-embracing pantheistic law. Freud also applied this universal law of Spinoza's pantheism to the human mind. If Spinozism is macro-pantheism, Melamed opines, Freudism is micro-pantheism always obeying certain immutable laws.

---

11. A General Selection of Freud Edited by John Rickmann, p. 50.
12. Ethic II 17-Schol.

Everything has its causes and it is always wise to understand it by these causes. All our actions in everyday life can be traced to their ascertainable causes. This is what Freud means by the term psychopathology. No mind is ever cursed, nor is it ever a haunt of evil spirits; all abnormality is due to its antecedent causes and should be searched out by every scientist. Thus Spinoza refrains from deriding our mental unhealthiness, and comes, like a doctor, to understand its entire scope by its various causes.

Spinoza's three basic affects are desire, joy and sorrow. He seems to have given primary importance to the first when he says that desire express the essence of man. And how he anticipates Freud when we come to know that the latter has also reduced all our emotions to the one basic desire of wish-fulfillment. As a remedy to our mental disturbances, Spinoza suggests arranging and connecting our passions and rechannelizing them. We have already pointed out how it comes to the Freudian thesis of sublimation. 'Sublimation', says Freud, 'eludes forces of frustration and affords way out for ego without involving repression'. It depends on the 'capacity of sexual instinct to change its object.' (Freud's pansexualism, we know, views all human instincts as only sexual instincts). With Spinoza, our faculty of reason gives us fortitude and strength of mind and frees us from all the mess of our passions. Reason is also the panacea for Freud. In a letter to Einstein, Freud writes, "The ideal condition would obviously be found in a community where every man subordinated his instinctive life to the dictates of reason."[13]

As long as Spinoza's world-picture will continue to dazzle humanity, so long will it continue to open up new portals of vision before all seekers of knowledge. As has been told by Eric Adikes, the non-scientific Spinoza has actually shaped the scientific process in Europe in the course of the last 150 years because of the overwhelming grandeur of his world picture. Highly interested in the 'whole' of things identified in God, Spinoza could influence the natural sciences, though he was never engaged in scientific labour as Descartes, Leibnitz and others. Let us say with Rattner that Spinoza has baffled the "crass contemporary contention that Truth instinctively shuns the philosophical study, and that she only favours

---

13. Sigmund Freud 'Why War'?

the laboratory or clinic where she freely comes and frankly discloses herself to the cold impersonal embrace of mechanical instruments."

In 1877, on the occasion of the bicentenary of Spinoza's death, Dr. Van Volten proposed to erect a statue at The Hague with subscriptions from home and abroad. The design of Frederic Hexamer was approved of by the Statue Committee and the monument was unveiled on the 14th of September, the same year.

Of late, a society has been started, after Spinoza, taking members from all over the world. This Spinoza Society has its central office in New York. They are carrying on serious studies of Spinoza from various aspects. Biosophy is the new name they have given to his philosophy. The Biosophical Review, devoted to character, peace and education, is regularly brought out by the society and has a worldwide circulation.

Human mind is dynamic and formative. So are also its products. Ideas become old as quick as they appear. So it will be unwise to weigh a great thinker of the 17th century with our modern scales. It is true that Spinoza's theory of causation has been for the time being nullified by the recent findings of physics, the quantum theory of Plank and Heisenberg's theory of Indeterminacy. But these are only the latest truths, not the truths for all time. No age has bound truth with its limits of standard. We, who have falsified the laws of the past century, stand similarly in the dock before the century that is ahead of us. In this sense, history is always alive with its great men. It is their approach to truth that has kept apace the progress of world's knowledge. All the thinkers of the past shine forever, with equal brilliance suggesting new ways and means to those who come after them. Did not Hegel take out but one sentence of Heraclitus and improve upon it his whole philosophy? Knowledge is never old, philosophy is never old, and science is never old. So also Spinoza is not.

4

Spinoza Reconsidered

It may not be superfluous to notice a few of the more common misapprehensions. [..] Even those which are so obvious and gross that it might appear impossible for any person of candor and intelligence to fall into them; since persons, even of considerable mental endowments, often give themselves so little trouble to understand the bearings of any opinion against which they entertain a prejudice, and men are, in general, so little conscious of this voluntary ignorance as a defect that the vulgarest misunderstandings of ethical doctrines are continually met with in the deliberate writings of persons of the greatest pretensions both to high principle and to philosophy.

—J.S. Mill, *Utilitarianism*, Ch. II

Benedict Spinoza belonged to the 17th century. That was three hundred years ago. Recently his students celebrated the 315th anniversary of his birth. What is the reason, then, that has prompted us to give our effort to the study of a thinker whose rightful place is only in the national museums? Our world is changing with the innumerable events that keep it moving forever. And with it, man and his ideas change, every epoch brings man out from the old scales and commends him to a new glossary of values. What have we, then, got to do with a thinker who happened to live three centuries back?

The history of philosophy keeps on record the long train of ideas that have shaken the world from its shackles. With these ideas is also associated a corresponding train of thinkers, both scientists and philosophers. They have each their venerable place in the galaxy of world changers and have each, when they have appeared, created in the world, the same sense of wonder and inspiration. The first man who discovered the usefulness of fire must have been hailed as sent by God by the cave-dwellers. In the making of civilization, the first man who taught the use of animal skin as a protection from cold is equally important as the modern inventor of pencillin. The modern thinker is the latest development of the Paleolithic man; the modern laboratory is the latest evolution from that of the first man who had started observing and speculating upon his small natural surroundings. Our age is only the uppermost rung in the history of thought. All the other rungs are equally important in as much as they support the one at the top and complete the ladder.

We have a mind; we think. What is more, most of the time, we think in advance. We never live only in the present. We have an inborn tendency to look into the things that are present before us. Our history owes its glory, not only to getting the truth about things, but also the truth of things.

Barring aside the geological periods of prehistoric age, our civilization is traced back to some thousand years. The relics of the old inhabitations tell us that our ancestors of those times also indulged in thinking. Philosophy is as old as human society. In the river plains of the Nile, the Euphrates and the Indus, in the solitary outskirts of the Greek city-states, also lived men and women, who also had thought seriously on the truth of things. From Thales who thought that the world was created from water, we have come, in the twentieth century, to the basic theory of electrons and positions. The problem is still there, exerting the strenuous efforts of all thinking men.

Yet what have we come to know? We have come to know a lot, yet an equal lot is still in the dark and is unknown. In every age, our men of science have been adding to our knowledge about nature but still the veil of mystery remains, hiding behind it vast prospects and possibilities. As Newton had said: "to myself I seem to have been only like a boy, playing on the sea-shore, and delighting myself in now and then finding a smoother pebble or a prettier shell than ordinary, whilst the great ocean of truth lay all undiscovered before me." This was the disillusionment, which had come to one of the masterminds of science. After knowing so much, we only know that we know still very little. As a modern thinker has put it, "There never was a time when so many people were so uncertain about so many things as at present." Chester Rowell writes, "Now we find ourselves in a whirlpool, in which nothing is fixed, not even the direction of the current in which we are floating."[1] Everything seems to be in an endless flux, betraying our facts and principles. The first thinker had started philosophizing on the 'why' of the world round him, and the same insoluble 'why' breaks all our effort, even after so many centuries. All our studies, to borrow from Amiel, only end in notes of interrogation.

But this is no taking a pessimistic outlook of things and resting content in skeptical inaction. We have come to know that the mystery of knowledge is great and colossal, and our efforts to unravel it must need be equally great and colossal too. The new age distinguishes itself in this respect that it comes to the door of knowledge only for the joy of it, but not, like the man of old to wonder at finding the world so big and vast and to shudder at his own insignificance. Max Plank visualizes in our age the beginning of a great renaissance.[2] But let us not digress further.

The gist is that though we have known many things, there is yet still much more to be known. From the infancy of thinking, different men have approached the same fundamental problems and have recorded down their own findings for posterity. Reaching the truth is not like reaching the land's end where we come also to our journey's end. Had it been like that, all our philosophy and science would have come to a standstill long before. No one has ever arrived at the final truth, and never has the world been fully satisfied so as not to think on the same problems. Hence, the only truth about our quest of truth is that its ways are varied and its approaches are many. Exactly as Mathew Arnold writes in his essay on Spinoza, "In my father's house there are many mansions."

Frederick Engels has written in his *Dialectic of Nature*: "In no case do we dominate Nature as the conqueror dominates an alien people, as though we are something standing outside nature, but that, on the contrary, since we with our flesh, blood and brain belong to Nature and are within Nature, we can only dominate it, in so far as we, unlike other beings, are able to discover and correctly apply her

---

1. *San Francisco Chronicle*—Aug '34.
2. Where is Science going? p. 64.

laws." We are already in Nature, her laws already exist, we only know as many of them as our knowledge reveals to us. Hence, whoever has entered the shrine of Nature with the inquisitiveness of a sincere thinker, his should be taken also as one of the many approaches made through the ages. Though we may differ from him in many points of interpretation, we must not, nevertheless, fail to give him our reverent recognition.

History of philosophy is full of the anthropopathic fallacy, that is, the fallacy of measuring another through one's own scale of values. This erroneous feature is present in almost all the departments of knowledge and this only shows how each one of us is full of his own passions and prejudices. Often our scholars, in their fanatic adherence to their own pet views of things, fail to do justice to another thinker and succeed only in so far as they show whether the latter's views agrees with his own. Hence, one is not surprised, if in the histories of philosophy, he reads only the author himself through the different schools of thinkers. 'Mine is the only way and all others are false,' is a crank in our diseased mind we all inherit from our savage forefathers. No system ever exhausts all the possibilities and so is not solely one's own. Knowing our incompleteness, we should also learn to tolerate other travellers in the same track, however their ideas may differ from ours. Pollock writes, "Science makes it plainer everyday that there is no such thing as a fixed equilibrium either in the world without or the mind within. So it becomes plain that the genuine and durable triumphs of philosophy are not in systems but in ideas.[3]

In all philosophical interpretation, writes Sir Radhakrishnan, "The right method is to interpret thinkers at their best, in the light of what they say in their moments of clearest insight."[4] In our interpretation of Spinoza, our criterion should also be this. We must try, not to find our own views read through him but to evaluate him in his own coins, just in determining the extent he could go in the direction of truth, and in his own way. Because, let us remember again, truth being so vast and extensive, we have to accept Spinoza's as one of the many approaches made to know the fundamental problems.

---

3. Pollock's Book, p. 406.
4. *My Search for Truth*, p. 15.

Spinoza, in his *Theologico-Politicus*, had demanded a historical study of the scripture. The same becomes still more imperative in philosophical studies too. Spinoza lived in a particular age, in a society of people having a particular bent of mind. Many things seem childish in him when we see him in contrast to our own age. Physics, philosophy and psychology have left away the ground far behind, where Spinoza had sown his seeds. But we can see him in his full and colourful worth only when we see him against the background of the 17th century and never of the modern age. To quote Radhakrishnan again, "To understand a great thinker we must have enough sympathy to imagine ourselves as standing in his place possessing his information, cherishing his beliefs, feeling his emotions."[5]

Words are the wise men's devices to deceive the common reader. Many of the problems of philosophy arise out of the sly quips and quibbles made use of by philosophers. The same words have been chosen by different thinkers to mean different things. God, Nature, Absolute etc. are some of the words, which have been given different meanings, and ranges of application by different philosophers. Hence, the Wittgensteinian method of philosophy emphasizes the linguistic analysis of philosophical questions 'Does God exist?' leads one to enquire the particular sense in which the word 'exist' is used. Students of philosophy, when they judge the thoughts of a philosopher, very often come across words of this sort. In their haste, they impute their own meanings to those words, forgetting the special sense in which they have been used. Thus they involve themselves in a dirty jugglery of problems.

There are many cases of like misjudging in Spinoza criticism made by various scholars. Many of them have forgotten the limited import in which Spinoza has used such words like God, Nature, Substance and Love. Love, as Spinoza understands by it, is perfect understanding with the joy that follows from it. His God is the Nature, or the eternal order of the existing things. Love of God means acquiring the perfect knowledge of the order of things. As regards this love of God of Spinoza, Melamed points out that his love of God is the lowest form of love and that communion with God always presumes a personal and a living God. He also writes in another place

5. *My Search for Truth*, p. 16.

that Spinoza's God can not be loved being without will or intellect. He cannot respond to love, which implies two living things. To look into the subtlety of things, it requires a sharp and sympathetic vision in which Melamed was perhaps lacking. So he reduces himself to the laughable plight of confusing his idea of love with that of Spinoza. Understanding through the data, which Spinoza has placed at our disposal, his love of God is quite intelligible. Instead of taking a fragmentary view of the order of things, and narrowing its scope only to one's own interest, we are to see the world as a much vaster structure, whose laws follow from a much greater necessity than our own. When we realize this truth, all our false notions of disorder and disharmony cease to exist, and we learn to live, not in ourselves only, but as a cooperating part of the greater universe. To come to this state of mental being is the intellectual love of God, as expounded by Spinoza. But to confound this with the amorous undertakings of our work-a-day life only proves the poverty of our thinking ability.

History of philosophy has its utility in so far as it helps us to build the philosophy of our own age. The old theories of world order, enunciated by the ancient philosophers, always give us the background where upon to form our own conceptions. It is, therefore, in no way wise to reject the old philosophers and their philosophies with indiscrimination. The right evaluation of our own ideas depends also on how we evaluate theirs.

II

Spinoza's world picture extends over the entire universe. The actuality, when taken in its complete denotation and connotation, is the God, Nature or Substance. Nature's law is universal and is equally meted out to determine the modes, man being one amongst them. To think of man outside the Law of Nature will be as preposterous as to think one universe within another. It is man who makes his own philosophy and so, he always wrongly draws everything to his interest, thinking, as it were, he is ruling the universe. But Nature is nothing to be conquered and subdued; we are, as we have seen from a passage from Engels quoted somewhere in these pages, only a part of Nature, fully representing its essence.

Spinoza's world picture has been accepted by many great minds of various spheres of knowledge as the one most realistic. But it remains equally obscure to those few, who would prefer to lie in their self-created cocoon of eternal doubt. From the very beginning they would have created, for the convenience of rejecting things, some idea patterns and would always labour unto the last to test all ideas in those patterns. And whichever does not fit in any of their pet types, they will condemn it as obscure and enigmatic. But as we know, great men of thought come to the world to break all the existing moulds and, hence, can never be fitted in any one of them.

The Substance has often been compared to the den of the lion, where there are many steps to, but few from. Everything belongs to God, the objection goes on and all have their existence in God. But where is the process by which things follow from God? Is not Spinoza's God an intellectual *cul de sac* wherein all the individual things mingle and lose their existence? But the fallacy of the notion lies in the fact that it suffers from betraying itself to anthropomorphism and can not but think the world in terms of man's daily dealings, of coming out and going in. It is a fancy to get metaphysical explanations on our worldly terms.

Melamed sees only death dominating all over the world of Spinoza. He shudders from the 'visions of a dead God'. Perhaps Spinoza's God does not fit into his fancy-woven types. He cannot understand a God without will and intellect. His pet God would have been an all-powerful and all-commanding God, cooperating with man and proving his valorous worth by superhuman exploits. To him, God should be free, free as a fretted child, perhaps to be propitiated by human offerings. Psychologically viewed, this tendency to make God the emblem of supreme lawlessness is a vestigial feature in man from those old days when man had no morals and codes of manner. Then he was no better than the other primate species upon earth. And till this age also, has remained that same instinct in man, the instinct to live at the cost of others, the modern 'survival by struggle'. Instinctively he imagines himself as the master of his environment, as one who has come to lord it over the Nature. Automatically the God of his conception is his substitute in heaven, the divine Tartar, who rules, who shows his power and who takes credit in maintaining His suzerainty over the world. In a world picture like this, God is the bully in the ideal realm and man is the bully in the actual realm. Hence, when Spinoza first brought down God from His ignobly high pedestal of the ruler and taskmaster and told that He is the world, the Tartar in everyman rose up in revolt.

Deity is the daughter of man's pride. The proud man has pictured God after the man par excellence. It is a model for him. Without a personal God ruling with the iron rod of reward and punishment, the common man finds himself abjectly dismembered. Without God, his life becomes, as it were, a ropeline without any support and stretched in eternal space. Hence man has so easily accepted a personal God and has pictured each of his activities, his love and hate, his virtue and vice, his good and bad as taking him near to or away from that personal God, his ideal.

Spinoza starts in a scientific way. A man of science cannot imagine God to have created the world and then to have stood with joyous surprise to see what He created. It may be convenient for a devotee but never convincing for a philosopher.

We do not know whence our life came. We know not also where are we to go after this earthly sojourn. All the theories of universe, so far advanced, are superstitious and fallacious. Looking for the causes of things, we are bound to stop at a point whose cause, again, cannot be found. It can only be assumed. No philosophy or no scientific doctrine has ever been without an assumption. In the words of William James, 'no philosophy can be more than a hypothesis'. A thinker has to accept a first cause. We are well aware of Plato's idea of the Good, Aristotle's Prime Mover, Stoics' Providence, Neo Platonists' Ineffable One, Berkeley's Father of Spirits, Kant's Moral Law and God (ands its sanction), Hegel's Absolute Idea, Eucken's Spiritual life, Herbert Spencer's Infinite and Eternal Energy. Bradley's Absolute Experience and James's Divine More. We know how the philosophy of each centers round an undefined idea. Even scientists like Newton and Galileo believed in God. And Descartes, the father of the modern spirit of doubt, called in God to solve all his doubts. Modern science also tends to assume that this world is the creation of a divine thinker. Coming to the East, we find the *Syāt-Vāda* of Jainism which always leaves a scope for exception in each of its certainties. In the Geeta, also, we read *Abyaktādeeni Bhutāni byaktamadhyāni...abyakta nidhamāni* "the origin of things remains unknown, so also their existence after extinction, only they are ascertainable by knowledge when they pass through this worldly phase."

The cause of the essence of things is yet unknown. Atoms, it is often supposed, behave as having minds too. The theory of indeterminacy has brought back causation to its own limited scope. The laws are only invulnerable in the physical realm. But the vast order of the universe prevails, whether or not we can bring it to the purview of our knowledge. This eternal existence, because in fact we do not know whether it had a beginning at all, has been divined by Spinoza. This is his Substance, the *Causa Sui*. The vast unknown, does, in no way, intervene in the laws of Nature which is nothing but God Himself. God and His laws are one and the same. This is the God of the scientist. The One Law operates in nature. The One Law holds the entire being in order and harmony. Man is only a little germ in it. He can know the world's laws only as far as a germ in the blood can know the whole system of blood circulation. This law that runs through all existence is surely great, it is the starting point of all our reasonings. Spinoza makes this his God. The individual modes are the existential manifestations of God.

Our senses, limited as their ranges are but false witnesses. They only give a fragmentary view of things, and taint all knowledge with the false notion of transference. Thus, we only know in part and consequently live in part also. It is only by enabling the intellect to take the whole view of things that we can come to the final realization of the eternal law pervading all existence. This is the intellectual love of God as envisaged by Spinoza. This is to attain a blessed state of mind, by reorientation of our affects, 'when we can know all things as one and subject to one law. This is Spinoza's God realization.

Spinoza starts with the assumption of God and ends with His realization. Bergson also started with biological mutations and variations and discovered his 'élan vital', the vital impetus. His intuitive leap is justified in so far as he is a poet, but philosophy becomes weakened by leaps of this kind. But Spinoza make no such leaps. He started with the vision of the world as it is, examined it as it is present to the senses, understood it, referred to it, to its cause and realized the excellence of seeing things *sub specie aeternitatis*. His adequate ideas, as distinguished from those inadequate, led us to the realization of the eternal essence of things, which is Spinoza's God. This God is known by the attainment of an ecstatic vision that knows, feels and visualizes only one Order, one Presence in all mind and body.

Spinoza's was not the helpless calling in of an external Deity as Descartes had done. The latter's doubts could only force him to posit a God, who came, as it were, on benefit of doubt. He was above and outside the things. He superimposed Himself on the universe. He is not to be realized, but to be accepted as the all-ruling Deity. But Spinoza started with this world, taking it to be the only order from which everything follows. All the individual things, with their different grades of existence, are in that order, not below or outside it. But, the question arises, if everything is in God, why can everyone not feel that he is in God? It is due to our mental affectations. So, in the last three parts of *Ethic*, Spinoza shows the way that leads us from what is to what might be.

After imagination and intellect, Spinoza introduces us to the third kind of knowledge, his scientific intuition. We have already seen how intuition is not a leap to the unknown. It is the steady way from understanding to realization. Thus, after coming through the process of perfect reason, we enter the realm of feeling, rather of immediate knowledge and realize God in all things and thoughts, in the world and in ourselves too. By this third kind of knowledge, we recognize ourselves in our divine credentials; we realize the Great Law in ourselves.

From geometry, from triangles and squares we have been led to God-realization. The ribald atheist has, in his own atheistic way, paved our way to the temple of the highest knowledge and wisdom. One wonders, if from the path of distinct fact, he has been betrayed to a labyrinth of dogma.

The unknown remains unknown, one would naturally complain. God remains and He is only traceable by the feeling of intuition. Then what did Spinoza actually give us?

The knowledge of the senses has never satisfied man. Otherwise philosophy would have stopped at empiricism. But, it has been felt by almost all the philosophers, there is something more than what is present to the senses. The beauty of a flower, the charm of a verse, the glory upon the human face are things, which are only felt. They can never be known as a problem of geometry. Our intellect gets a set back from knowing the reality in those things. Thus Spinoza leaves the ground to intuition whereby alone can God be realized. But by so doing, he never ignores reason, but allocates to it its rightful functions.

The dogma remains. It remains today also. It will remain the same as long as we are too peevish to leave our skeptical bent of mind. The world is to be understood in its entirety, taking account of everything, including those that lie beyond the ken of our senses, even if the skeptic rejects them as dogma. By whatever name we may call them, our world will never be complete without them. Kant had to admit a place for insoluble antinomies in his first *Critique*. One cannot blink aside things, only because one does not understand them. As Paulsen writes, 'Dogmatic negation is no less presumptuous than positive dogmatism.' We agree with the French philosopher, Renouvier when he says: "Any philosophy which does not, at the outset, take account of the uncertainties, variations and contradictions arising out of it; but which entertains the illusion of getting rid of them by suppression, is, let us say, a bravado, a pure childishness to which we should not stoop."

The ancient man began with wonder and his philosophy was the enchanted acceptance of the Divine rulership. His ethics was submission to fear and propitiation. The age of science diverted man's inclination to the other extreme, the extreme of cold reason and obstinate negation. Neither is the right way. The golden middle is neither complete superstition nor self-complacency pure and simple. The skeptics do not do any service to philosophy by deriding others as dogma. They only create another Diogenean tub for themselves and shut up inside and fancy they know everything. Spinoza's excellence was here, in giving everything its right place in the universe. He welcomed imagination as long as one was conscious of it, he gave reason its proper place too, giving an 'all clear' to science, but what is more, he raised the power of intellect to intuition and made God realizable by love, though powerless our reason may be. For having done this, he can never be blatantly denied as a dogmatist. Melamed writes that Spinozism is religiosity and mysticism couched in philosophical terms. He further adds that only a mystic can accept Spinoza's Substance, because it is mysticism and not philosophy. Many also have called him a dogmatist. And if so, let us borrow the expression from Hocking 'he is a dogmatist devoted to reason'.

Spinoza's God is self-determined. He acts under no blind will but from the necessity of His own eternal essence. This is the only world. God is not a sorcerer who confounds the world with magic specimens of creation. We are inclined to picture God as a super-powerful magician because we always think of Him as being outside us. But Spinoza's God is the creation itself, rather He is the things begotten as they are. Hence, to imagine a better representation of things than what has been is to belittle God's power. God could have created no other world other than what has been. But Spinoza warns us, "In no way do I subject God to fate, but I conceive that everything follows with inevitable necessity from the nature of God."[6] In this sense, God is the only free cause, determined not by any outside agent, but by Himself. In the poetic words of Tagore, "Where is Deliverance? Our master Himself has joyfully taken upon Him the bonds of Creation." God has no other option but to exist as He does.

Bergson's world is all movement. Spinoza's world is all existence. The former is always becoming; the latter, being. In this respect Plato and Spinoza can be differentiated from the other line of thought, that of Heraclitus and Bergson. Many scholars complain that Spinoza's world is static and his God is a dead one. The only reply to these insinuations would be that Spinoza's world is much bigger than the world of snapping and changing moments. It is the greater harmony which embraces, into it, all flash and flux. In the words of Gunn, "For Spinoza, change is but an aspect of reality, a reality that abides. Behind all changes, there lies a permanent enduring Reality of which change is a manifestation." But this Reality, it should be remembered, does not deny action. A free man is a man of action, never of passion. Activity is an essential character of Reality, according to Spinoza. We know a thing adequately only as far as we act. In the explanation of the third definition of the second part of *Ethic*, Spinoza uses the word 'conception' rather than perception, because the term perception seems to indicate that the mind is passive in its relation to object. The very import he gives to an idea which, when defined, shows us the action of mind. Spinoza describes Substance and Attributes as powers and in *Ethic* (I 17 and II 3) Substance or God is identified with power. In his letters,[7] he refutes Descartes's matter as inert extension. For him, extension or matter is

---

6. Letter no. 75.
7. Letters no. 81 and 82.

essentially physical energy. "Extension is the 'power to produce' motion and rest or kinetic and potential energy."[8]

Another point of contention in Spinoza is that he banishes teleology from philosophy. God has no end before Him. He acts from the necessity of His own existence. Then what is the purpose for this existence? That cannot be explained. The germ cannot ascertain the purpose of blood circulation. Spinoza denies all finalism, as it is humanly understood. Being only a mode in the eternal order, we cannot ascertain whereto we are leading. It comes very near to the Hindu theory of 'Leela' or Cosmic Dance. The 'Life Force', has the term as been coined by Bernard Shaw, goes on baffling all our restricted visions and designs. But this does not deny future; only it affirms that the human mind cannot know it. Nature is not mad, it does not drive to nowhere, but in the words of Shakespeare, 'there is method in this madness'.

Spinoza's system of realizing the self in the Substance is not devoid of any teleology; but it is, as Joachim puts it, an 'immanent teleology'. On our path of realization, it is never distinct to us as geometry that we are being led to a God-union, but the elevated self always finds its aspiration culminated in the *amor intellectualis Dei*, when we see only the One.

III

The common man spurns all submission. By nature he is averse to believe that he is only a manifestation among many manifestations and not the only one.

Hence, it was not accidental that the first man painted himself a monarch in the order of creation; the sun and the moon shone for him, the monsoon winds brought rain only for himself, his God was also his all-powerful collaborator. This idea of isolated superiority was so deeply ingrained in human thinking that when Darwin allied man with the long line of evolving species beginning from the amoeba, his theory raised a hue and cry of protest from all available quarters. The way of knowledge and experiment may show the other way, but it

---

8. *Short Treatise*, p 120.

was supposed to be a heresy to dethrone man from his position of the all determinator, for whom everything moved and had its being.

Spinoza preached universalism in creation. Though granting various grades of existence, he brought all existence into the largest comprehensible whole, the Substance. Nothing is outside the Substance. Quoting Ingersoll, "The universe is all there is, or was or will be. It is both subject and object, contemplator and contemplated, creator and created, destroyer and destroyed, preserver and preserved, and hath within itself all causes, modes, motions and effects."[9] All follow from God, beginning from the smallest microcosm to man. The universe does not exist for man. God is never the cooperator with man in his efforts for building a world for himself. Man is only an aspect, a mode, an individual thing.

Human insolence found it hard to stand Spinoza's universalism. Man can never be made to fall in line with the lesser creation and whoever does it, must be a heretic and his philosophy must be false. Hence, Spinoza also has been charged with the sin of belittling man, of making him only an insignificant mode. Spinoza's God, they demur, is eternal and infinite and when man becomes only a part of it, his individuality is lost. Philosophically this problem can be stated as the one of the relation between the universal and the particular. All particular is God. As has been pointed out, is not Spinoza's God akin to that mysterious den of the lion, where all foot-prints lead to but never come out of it? Cousin writes: "Thus in the philosophy of Spinoza, man and nature are mere phenomena, simple attributes of sole and absolute Substance."[10] In the footnote on the same page, he continues, "Far from being an atheist, of which he is accused, Spinoza professes so strongly, the sentiment of God, that he loses the sentiment of man." "This temporary and limited existence, everything that is finite, seems to him unworthy of the name of existence, and for him, there is no true being but the eternal being."

Melamed becomes furious at Spinoza's underrating the particular, especially man. In his fury he degrades religion to helpless submission to the unknown, whose laws cannot be understood and yet must be carried on. He accuses Spinoza as a religionist in this

9. Prose-Poems and Quotations, p. 142.
10. History of Modern Philosophy. Vol. II: p. 79.

distorted sense. "True religiosity," he writes "is not an understanding of how God is correlated to man and to the world, but the feeling of man's insignificance in the cosmos, giving birth to a state of meekness, humbleness and pity. Only when man is crushed and overwhelmed by the thought of his insignificance in this vast universe, does he become truly religious. These feelings are as present in Spinozism as they are in Buddhism."[11] It seems that Melamed has not been able to grasp the true spirit in Spinozism, much less in Buddhism.

At another place, Melamed continues, "Most of the thinkers have exalted man. Spinoza, while reducing man only to a modus of insignificance, brought a shock to ethics. Man, being only a mode, is only a whim-product of blind destiny, moving without any goal. This conception has made Spinoza the most contested figure.[12] Aldous Huxley also ridicules Spinoza for having made man a worm that matters little in the infinite universe of things.

Subject to critical judgement, Melamed's estimate of Spinoza suffers from shallow understanding. First, he commits the greatest blunder of taking Spinoza's universe as being created, as if some 'blind destiny, moving without any goal' goes on creating things out of nothing.' This conception would bring down Spinozism to sheer fatalism. Spinoza's man, Melamed remarks, is a 'whim-product'. The very term 'product' has no meaning in Spinoza's explanation of the universe. The world did never begin to be, it is. Existence is not the product of God, it is God, the Substance or Nature. And thus understood, man is not a mode in the sense that he is an insignificant whim-product, but the he is God. Those critics who separate the forms of existence from Spinoza's God, kill the very spirit of his philosophy and risk the crime of mispainting it.

This sort of argument, as Melamed gives, reminds one of the Christian dogmas of assuming a God who suddenly makes up His mind to create things. "Let there be light," the Lord is supposed to have said and there was light. The last and the best thing God created, according to the Bible, was man and He made him the ruler upon earth. This theory of the exaltation of man was only the reflection of

11. *Spinoza and Buddha*, p. 2.
12. *Ibid*, p. 214.

the primitive notion that still lingered in men's minds. Spinoza expurgated all such Gods from philosophy and took existence, eternal and infinite, as the only God, the only dispenser. The past, the present and the future commingled themselves in the One Substance that was eternal. All forms of existence were made divine.

Likewise man also became divine. There is no God above the earth, always to be feared and propitiated by worship. Man himself is God, God is to be realized by reason and intuition in one's self. Man is not alone in this world, extorting allegiance towards himself from a hostile crowd of created things. He is bound with all existence in his very essence and thus becomes large by being a part of the larger whole. He is rather a focus than a means in the realm of existence. Coming to Indian philosophy, life is immense *prāno virāt yah cha, asmin ākāse, yah cha asmin ātmani, tejomayamrtamayah pūrusa sarbānubhūr-*. The one *Téjomaya Pūrūsha* is not only in space but also in our own souls.

Man is glorified when he bears in himself the essence of God too. Spinoza's critics fall short of this comprehension and hence they complain that man is left only as an insignificant mode in Spinoza's creation. The difference lies only in the manner in which we take the things to be. The critics fancy that man can be significant only by becoming the ruler upon earth or not at all. The idea of the survival by struggle still gnaws at the very fibres of their brains and they cannot think of a friendly universe of being, where all the forms of existence including man constitute the essence of God. Spinoza brought down divinity to this earth below and with it, existence was dignified par excellence. God is not a far off thing to be pined for by imperfect and sinful souls, He is to be realized within by the enlightenment of the mind. Man is not to be afraid of the deadly wrath of God of whom he does not possess any knowledge, but, on the other hand, to live cheerfully by knowing the truth about his emotions and to find himself sub specie aeternitatis. This is the consecrated picture of man as given by Spinoza. Man's significance is not foreign to him. He is inlaid with divine magnificence. Only it waits for a right revelation when the coverings are unfolded.

Improving upon his miscomprehension, Melamed goes on to show that Spinoza was a pessimist. Man is lost in the *mêlée* of created existence. He is no superior to other things of creation. His future and his prospect are no better than those of a piece of stone, as both equally express the essence of God. Melamed justifies himself by putting against Spinoza the contrast from the Bible, which goes to the farthest lines in exalting man. "Judaism lays stress upon man [...] the Bible is a book of man. It gives the picture of a future, a hope of gradual evolution. The past was bad, the present miserable, but there is, in the future, a great day of reckoning, the birth of a Messiah... The Jew is thus optimistic. Spinoza came and obliterated all his hopes, eliminated the Messiah." Cousin becomes so sure about the pessimism of Spinoza that he accounts for the same by the tragic events of the latter's life: "He lived in a suburb of the city, where gaining, as a polisher of glass, the little bread and milk necessary for his subsistence, hated, repudiated by the men of his community; suspected by all others, detested by all the clergy of Europe [...] escaping persecutions only by concealment..., passing along in this world without wishing to stop in it, never dreaming of producing any effect upon it, or of leaving any trace upon it."

These charges are most refuted when we consider how under Spinoza's system the particulars are highly dignified. They give up their isolated individuality and regain it by forming a part of an all pervasive whole. Man becomes a part of God, a being full of sacred significance. And what is more, the power of realizing this divinity lies within the capacity of every mind. Man has the potential requirements of attaining full knowledge. What can be more optimistic than this prophetic assurance about the greatness of man? One can look for support to more than one places in the *Ethic*: "the human mind possesses an adequate knowledge of the eternal and infinite essence of God."[13] Also, "A free man thinks of nothing less than of death, and his wisdom is not a meditation upon death, but upon life."[14] Everyone has the power, partly at least, if not absolutely, of understanding clearly and distinctly himself and his affects and consequently of bringing it to pass that he suffers less from them." The mind suffers from its attachment to emotions that are transitory, but yet there is a hope of redemption in that it can be so prepared to turn passions into actions and thus rejoice in them. So those who pretend to see only pessimism in Spinoza, betray their own passions

13. Ethic II. 47.
14. Ethic IV. 47.

and prejudices. They cannot prepare themselves for a sympathetic understanding of the philosopher. In their sick hurry to find their own preconceived thoughts in another thinker, they make even the clearest truths remain oblivious to them. Committing this basic error in judgement, they are deprived of all the truth lying in a philosophical treatise. Here, in their study of Spinoza, the error lies in wrongly valuing Spinoza's peculiar type of pantheism, and as they have misread it, they are also helpless to detect the other truths that follow from it.

Spinoza's philosophy was not for the pleasure of man, nor of any mundane authority. Truth was his only master, he served it so sincerely and did not scruple to come to any conclusion as was demanded by truth. Though obedient and true to his master, he could not be loved by a man and human authority like Leibnitz. To Spinoza, man was only secondary to truth and not vice versa. And so also was he as much optimistic only as his pursuit of truth could allow him. Quoting Rattner, "Spinoza was no incurable optimist, or Leibnitzian Pangloss who believes this is, for man, the best of all possible worlds. To be humanly idealistic, it is by no means, necessary to be superhumanly utopian. But neither is Spinoza a shallow Schopenhauerian pessimist. Spinoza's realistic appraisal of man's worldly state is entirely free from all romantic despair. This world is no more the worst than it is the best of all possible worlds for man. Although man cannot completely alter his evil state, he can better it."[15]

Spinoza speaks of no doctrine of original sin. Nor does he brag of presenting a magic wand to man, whereby he can instantaneously change all dross to gold. He draws out a perfect and comprehensible world system where all forms of being assume divine essence. The divinity is brought to this earth, to the reach of those who can make the necessary preparations for it. The mind is also given the power of knowing reality, of realizing itself in the eternal order of things. This is not salvation as is ordinarily thought of, nor redemption by any miraculous escape, it is being immortal by virtue of the fullest comprehension. This optimistic vein has been struck by Robert Ingersoll, in his natural simplicity of style in the following words; "In

15. Philosophy of Spinoza, p. LI.

this, there is all hope. This is a foundation and a star. The Infinite is the All. Without the All, the Infinite cannot be. I am something; without me, the infinite can not exist."[16]

IV

Spinoza's universe is determined. Even his God or Substance is devoid of will. He cannot work under free will. He is but governed by the laws of His eternal essence and existence. It is misreading God's power to say that He could create anything He pleased. In the *Ethic*, Spinoza has elucidated how in giving free will to God, we restrict His omnipotence. All powerful as He is, He has made things manifest in the only possible world which is existent.

Creation is not a miracle, it is not the card-tricks of an unknown sorcerer. There is law in this universe and but for this law, existence would have been only subject to superstition. Spinoza's motive was to prove that the world exists by science, and not by magic. Hence, he upheld the opinion that Nature is not free, but determined. There is order everywhere, in space, in the process of thought and in the movement and change of all forms of existence. An aggregate of unconnected events can never explain our world.

Spinoza's theory of determinism was the natural outcome of his scientific outlook of mind. As a rationalist, he saw, over the crowd of events, the law that governed them. A life of reason is impossible if the world is a victim of chance. In a lawless world would man forever sink in abysmal ignorance and his life would be nothing nobler than a doll's dance pulled by the strings of a capricious Deity. But if the things are all determined by necessity, that is, have their existence governed by certain discernible laws, science and a considerable extent of scientific control is possible for man.

But this doctrine, by which Spinoza meant to make man more sure and powerful in life, was very easily misread by the contemporary wise men, both in and outside the clergy. People objected to it on the ground that it robbed man's life of all moral and religious value. Science was yet lying enfeebled in the grips of

16. Prose Poems and Selections, p. 142.

theology, and hence the most scientific theory of Spinoza was very quickly resented by all who were concerned.

But the anti-determinists wildly confuse a perverted determinism of ends with a scientific determinism of means. Henry Oldenburg, one of Spinoza's persistent correspondents, was a prey to this confusion. When Spinoza told him that things are governed by the laws of creation, he was shocked to find the world divested from all freedom, as if the 'toothbrush I shall buy tomorrow will be determined by the stellar dust of aeons ago!' Tooth brush is a commodity in the market and its purchase and sale are governed only by the laws of business transaction. Spinoza's doctrine of necessity maintains that all events are determined by their proper causes, not that 'everything is immediately caused by some antediluvian event.' It is true that I and the toothbrush would not exist if the stellar dust would not have existed. But one should not draw from it the preposterous conclusion that the stellar dust existed so that I might exist today to purchase a toothbrush tomorrow, nor that I and the toothbrush exist today because the stellar dust of old should have a final purpose. Giving another simpler instance, when I pluck a flower, the movement of my hand is subject to the laws of dynamics; the muscular strain is due to certain laws of physiology. But the plucking of flower itself by me is never determined. Neither I existed so that the flower might be plucked by me at the particular moment, nor the flower existed so that I might pluck it. In the latter case it is fatalism, which can never be attributed to Spinoza's doctrine of determinism. As Rattner puts it, "Only when causality is perversely teleological is determinism fatalistic. Fatalism is the result only when the ends of activity are necessarily but arbitrarily determined. But when causality is not arbitrarily teleological or when only the nature of things, the instruments or means of activity are necessarily determined, the determinism involves no fatalism at all." Spinoza's determinism, in another way, finds its support in the doctrine of the uniformity of nature. Without this law, all scientific thought would have been impossible. If nature acted merely by freaks, its future movements could never be speculated with certainty. Only because we believe that the world will exist tomorrow by the same laws of existence as it exists today, do we think and generalize for the future."

Of late, James's philosophy of contingency and Bergson's theory of eternal change seem to shake the consistency of determinism.

Plank's Quantum theory and Heisenberg's theory of Indeterminacy establish that in the microscopic universe, there is a certain scope for freedom. But this indeterminateness is only confined to the movements of the lighter atoms, the ultimate constituents of matter. But as the originators of indeterminism themselves have shown,[17] this indeterminacy is negligible in the macroscopic world. So that in processes such as astronomical movements, physiological changes and the rest, determinism may be said to rule. The astronomical rules determine the movement of the stars, the physiological rules determine the process of the body machine, and the physical rules determine the nature of a thing. Spinoza's determinism, as we have seen it opposed to fatalism, is not refuted by the theory of indeterminacy. As Patrick puts it, "Determinism is not disproved; it is simply transcended. Its language does not fit the situation. Neither are such words as indeterminism and libertarianism particularly happy [...] Let the traditional Martian visitor come to Earth and say to man, 'Are you free?' 'No', would be the answer, 'we are hampered'. Are all your movements controlled and determined? 'Nonsense! No! we are striving for certain ends and gaining them with difficulty'.[18] In lieu of the expression, 'freedom of the will' which so often misleads us, Patrick suggests more fitting substitutes such as 'freedom of the self' and 'freedom of the mind'.

Let us come down to Spinoza's God or Nature. It was only due to his scientific bent of mind that he divorced all will from God. Only when we assume an anthropomorphic all-ruling God, then can we posit a will for Him. But Spinoza's God is Existence itself. Things are not created by God in His transcendental laboratory, they are God. And this God is governed by immutable laws. But we must remember that God and His laws are one and the same with Spinoza. Summarizing, God is governed or determined by His own laws, He acts from the eternal necessity of His own essence, that is, He is self-determined or free. "God who is absolutely free, has, at the same time, necessary existence, understanding and operation, that is, He exists understands and operates from the necessity of His own nature. For undoubtedly God operates with the same necessity by which He

17. Plank, Philosophy of Physics, Ch. II.
18. Introduction to Philosophy, p. 310.

exists; as therefore He exists from the necessity of His own nature, He also acts, that is, He acts with absolute freedom."[19] "In no way do I subject God to fate, but I conceive that everything follows with inevitable necessity from the nature of God."[20] Thus Spinoza's determinism makes God free by making Him self-determined. Teleological fatalism has nothing to do with Spinoza's necessity. Only anthropomorphic dogmas such as the Christian theology suffer from such aberrations. Spinoza's is the scientific determinism in the realm of Nature. This is why Rattner calls Spinoza, "the only thoroughly emancipated, the only thoroughly modern and scientific philosopher that ever lived." And he is, much more certainly, "the only thoroughly emancipated, the only thoroughly modern and scientific ethicist that ever lived."

Here comes the ever-enigmatic question; if everything in this world, including God Himself is determined, then how can we justify evil upon earth? If man has no power over his mental volitions, then how a thief can be held responsible for theft or how the boastful man for his lust? This brings complete anarchy in the moral universe when all freedom is banished. An action, in order that it may be moral, must needs be a voluntary one so that the person who does it can be held legally responsible for its consequence. The dogmatic theorizers of every religion have broken their heads with this problem of evil. They have started with the anthropomorphic conception of an all-pure and all-virtuous God, to whom our vices can never be attributed. Hence in every religion, evil and vice has either been personified with the wicked Satan or has been transferred to man. Zoroastrianism fancies a perpetual fight between the Ahura Marzda and Ahriman, the Gods, respectively, of good and evil, with victory always changing sides. In the Christian apologetics, man has been given the power of 'free' man so that God's perfect goodness might not be contaminated. But the 'freedom' of this conception is not to enable man to live virtuously, but to enable him to sin. Man is not 'free' either to live virtuously or sinfully, but he is only 'free' to sin! And the age, which already lay diseased with these distorted notions of 'free will' could not, without

19. Tractatus Politicus, Ch. II. 7.
20. Letter no. 75.

revolting; swallow the pill of scientific necessity that Spinoza served through his philosophy.

And what is this freedom? Does free life mean a life of unbridled passions without any sensible control? What would happen to that man who is absolutely free in the theologist's sense of the term, free to do anything and everything he likes? This is not freedom, this is insensible license, absolute libertinism. A 'free' man in this sense becomes more wretched than a slave.

Rousseau, a century after Spinoza, conceived of absolute freedom. It made man a slave to ignorance and brought about anarchy in society. Epicurus of old was also an advocate of freedom and indeterminism. The clamorous moralists of the middle ages also raised a cry for this free will, which, they believed, was the very foundation of all morality and religion. But rightly viewed, the freedom of this perverted type makes all morality shaken and disintegrated, far less it stabilizes it. No morality can be forced upon a mind that is averse to all responsibility. If man has a free will instead of a determinate nature, he can never be relied to take any responsibility. Education will be of no avail if our minds are absolutely free. There will be complete anarchy of the "jungle," and perhaps the unthinkable havoc, quite natural to follow, when this 'back to nature' slogan is accomplished, will be the fate of the world.

Responsibility not irresponsibility, reliability not unreliability, certainty not uncertainty, is the necessary condition of all human morality. As Joad says, "The achievement of freedom is the beginning of responsibility."[21] What is wanted is, according to Rattner, a firm will not a 'free' will. Watter Siegmeister calls it the 'internal freedom' without which all external freedom carries no value. "True freedom," he writes, "in its highest sense, means consciousness and obedience to, not only the laws of logic, but to the higher revelations of intuition. […] Then only is man in harmony with nature and then only are true freedom and happiness attained."[22]

Take for instance, the freedom enjoyed by Mahatma Gandhi. His working day was strictly routine. The time he would take in walking, sleeping, taking food and spinning was fixed to the minute. He could

21. Philosophy of Our Times, p. 343.
22. Spinoza Quarterly: Tercentenary Issue, p. 104.

not smoke a cigarette. He could not take meat, eggs, this and that. He was not free to go on a holiday when he pleased. He was not free to meet his friends and associates except in appointed hours. He was not free to speak as he pleased, eat as he pleased and dress as he pleased. Everything had its due and restricted place in his life, neither less nor more than that. Should not we, then, call him a free man? Truly speaking, he was the freest man of all we know. Having submitted himself to the rules of health, of religion and of reason, he had attained the largest amount of freedom of mind. Cutting up the external freedom to the minimum, he was internally the freest. Being self-determined, he ceased to be passion's slave. He was a free man in the sense that he acted under the necessity of his own reason. Spinoza writes, "I make freedom consist not in a free decision of the will, but in free necessity." He makes will and intellect the one and the same thing. Will, to him, is the mere affirmation or negation of taking a decision accordingly as necessity demands.

Here a clear margin can be drawn between necessity and slavery. A man acts from the necessity of the dictates of his own reason. But a slave plays himself into the hands of another, over whom he has no control. Freedom and necessity are never contradictory terms; only freedom and slavery may be so. In the words of Rattner, "Freedom is not opposed to necessity or determinism; Freedom consists not in absolute indetermination, but in absolute self-determination." The Indian equivalents of the term 'free' comes nearer to its true philosophical import. *Swādheena* and *swatantra* literally mean self-dependent, never independent. Spinoza writes: "The true slave is he who is led away by his pleasures and can neither see what is good for him, nor act accordingly; he alone is free who lives with free consent under the entire guidance of reason."[23]

The charge is brought against Spinoza that by his theory of determinism he annihilates his entire theory of ethics. Morality does not mean anything to the man who is devoid of all voluntariness. But, as has been already clear, this is but a false accusation. Spinoza's determinism only means self-determinism in ethics, never the absence of all freedom. In the fifth part of the *Ethic*, Spinoza speaks of the 'power of reason', 'showing the extent and nature of the authority

---

23. *Tractatus Theologico-Politicus.*

which it has over the affects in restraining them and governing them.' Recognizing this power of reason to restrain and govern our passions, is a clear indicator that Spinoza does not picture the human mind as imbecile. At another place Spinoza writes, 'Everyone is allowed by the highest right of nature to do that which he believes contributes to his own profit.'"[24] Expressions as these entirely ward off all suspicion that Spinoza's man is amoral. It is criminal to conclude that Spinoza, by his determinism, made of man an amoral automation.

The same error was committed by Oldenberg who, even to the last, could not understand Spinoza's determinism. In letter no. 75, Spinoza had written that "men are inexcusable before God for no other reason than that they are in the power of God Himself as clay in the hand of the potter." Commenting, Oldenberg wrote, "If we human beings are, in all actions, moral as well as natural, as much in the power of God as clay in the hand of the potter, with that right can any one of us be blamed for acting in this or that way, when it was absolutely impossible for him to act otherwise?"[25] Spinoza wrote back: "What I said in my previous letter, that we are in the power of God as clay in the hand of the potter, I wanted to be understood in this sense, namely, that no one can blame God because He has given him an infirm nature or an impotent mind. For it would be just as absurd for a circle to complain that God has not given it the properties of a sphere, as for a weak-minded man to complain that God has denied him strength and the true knowledge and the love of God, and that He has given him a nature so weak that he can not restrain or moderate his desires." And again, "Men are excusable and nevertheless lack blessedness and be tormented in many ways. For a horse is excusable for being a horse and not a man, nevertheless it must be a horse and not a man.... He who is unable to control his desires and to restrain them through fear of the laws, although he must be excused for his weakness, is nevertheless unable to enjoy peace of mind and the knowledge and love of God, but necessarily perishes.'"[26]

---

24. *Ethic*, p. 242.
25. Letter no. 77.
26. Letter no. 78.

Thus, though our life is determined by God, our will to be better or to be ethically stronger is entirely left to us. We can never justify our lapses and shortcomings by pretending that we are determined so by God. This reminds one of the funny story woven round the Phoenician merchant-philosopher Zeno who believed that all our thoughts, our acts, our very lives are the instruments of Destiny. One day Zeno had flogged his slave for some offence. "Pray, forgive me, master," begged the slave, "for by your philosophy I have been destined from all eternity to commit this offence." "Quite true", replied Zeno, "But by the same philosophy, I have been destined from all eternity to flog you for this offence." Because God is omniscient and hence is aware of our sins, it is not true necessarily that He is responsible for all our sins. Thus also says Milton, when he writes:

> [...] If I foreknew,
> Foreknowledge had no influence on their fault,
> Which had no less proved certain unforeknown.[27]

The free soul delights in accepting bonds. Our salvation lies in self-determination. "I shall call that free which is determined by itself alone." In the words of Gunn, Spinoza "leaves no opposition between freedom and necessity. Men are not born free as Rousseau fancied, but men can be free. We are never more free than when we are impelled to a thing because we judge it to be true and good. Self-determination does not annihilate but increases freedom.

This is also the most modern explanation of freedom. W. M. Horton writes, "We are never so much at the mercy of external circumstance as when we are in a state of indecision; never so free as when we have bound ourselves by a decision. Again, the limitations that we take upon ourselves when we assume some specific place in the social order, are not at all hampering limitations, in making ourselves the willing servants of society we become masters of circumstances as no solitary Promethean individualist could ever be."[28]

---

27. *Paradise Lost*, Book III, pp. 117-119.
28. *A Psychological Approach to Theology*, p. 62.

Julian Huxley has also said: "Certain it is, that the freedom of the will is in a way paradoxical; for the more disciplined and efficient the mind and the more clearly and fully the alternatives are envisaged, the quicker and more effortless is the choice,—and yet the greater is the sense of freedom and spontaneity in the choice. It may well be that the controversy will turn out to be an unreal one, based on a false logic in the definition of freedom; and that what we call freedom consists essentially in the power of envisaging a number of 'alternatives together in the mind while mere arbitrariness and non-determinate choosing, which is often thought to be the essence of free-will, is really something which can not exist and can indeed really be thought at all."[29]

By a free society, Middleton Murrgy means a self-disciplined society. He writes, "Absolute freedom is absolute nihilism. The only true and enduring freedom is that which is achieved by self-limitation, and obedience to a universal law whose validity is self evident to human reason. If the intelligence of a free society is so warped that it can not discover this law, and its instinct so perverted that it can not accept it, the free society will perish."[30]

Spinoza had perfectly understood the human mind. Like a sympathetic doctor, he could well-ascertain what freedom really means to man. Thus only he could be able to present before man the best possible ethics. His was neither a Utopia nor a document of despair weeping at the weakness of man. His *Ethic* was drawn out to meet the needs of the human nature as it is. Let us reiterate with Rattner that Spinoza was the only thoroughly modern and scientific ethicist that ever lived.

V

Isā-bāsyamidam sarbamyatkimcha Jagatyām jagat-whatever there is changeful in this ephemeral world, all that must be enveloped by the Lord—this first verse of the *Iśavāsyopanisad* proclaims the oneness of God. This oneness or non-duality is the essence of Indian philosophy. Though a certain section of thinkers have held the

---

29. *Religion without Revelation*, p. 89.
30. From his article in *World Review*, October 1947.

dualistic view, yet the former has always remained more prominent and representative.

Sa pargāchchukramakāyamabranam asnābiram sūddham apāpabiddham 'He is everywhere, without a body, without muscles and without the taint of sin, radiant, whole and pure'. He is *kabih, maneesee, swayambhū* and *paribhu* 'seeing, knowing all, self-existent and all compassing." This Sa is Spinoza's substance, Nature or God. He pervades all things, both great and small.

The universe, as it appears to the ordinary eyes, is dual in character. The ideal and the real, God and Lucifer are the dual expressions by which we know Existence. Then how is it that it is enveloped by One God, be it Substance or Nature?

Spinoza says, our senses are false witnesses. Our view of things is nothing but subjective. We always see ourselves, our thoughts and our ideas through a thing and fancy that we have seen the thing. But the moment we begin to sense things genuinely free of passions, prejudices and narrow limitations, the idea of Existence soon presents itself before us as one, operating under the one law. Drawing a simile from Shamkara, the appearances are like the many moons appearing on the surface of water when it is stirred. But in reality, there is only one moon. He writes,

Éka éka cha bhutātmā bhuté bhuté byabasthitā
Ékadhā bahūdhā chāpi drshyaté jalachandra bat.

'The one resides in all things; like the moon in the water; it only appears to be many. Through the attributes of thought and extension, we see substance in multitudinous forms. These attributes are not the many divisions of God, they are the different aspects through which we come to know God, who, otherwise is One."

Indian philosophy is often misinterpreted that the world of existence in itself is *Māyā* and Reality lies outside it. On the contrary, the Upanisads, when they contemplate the one Brahma that pervades all, gives to everything its divine dignity. Water, fire, the trees and the rocks, in the eyes of one who has realized, become Brahma and cease to be mere appearances. Brahma is there, without a doubt, in the world. It exists, it gives light to all and makes them manifested *tameba bhānta anūbhāti sarbam tasyabhāsā sarbamidam bhibhāti* God is there in everything, only those with eyes of illusions cannot know Him to be there. The Maya is not any defect of the Brahma Himself, it is rather the defect of the eyes that look at Him. To bring in another simile of Shamkara, we throw a bamboo stick on the surface of water in a tank and fancy that the water is divided. But in truth, the water is one and undivided, and the truth becomes clear to us as soon as the bamboo stick is removed. Similarly the world appears to be many because our perverted vision stands in our way and no sooner the vision becomes pure and untainted, than we realize the One. Shankara writes in *'Hastāmalakam, ghanāchhannadṛstih ghanāchhannamarkam, yathā miṣprabham manyaté chātimūdhah tathā baddhabadbhāti yah mūdhadṛṣṭéh sa nityopalabdhiswarūpah ahamatma.*

'In a cloudy day we wrongly say that the sun has been covered up by the clouds. The truth would be, our eyes have been covered up by the clouds. The sun shines no doubt and is visible to that part of the earth where there are no clouds. Only our eyes cannot see the sun as the clouds intervene. Yet we fancy that the clouds have kept the sun hidden from our eyes. In the same way, God can never be enveloped by *Māyā*, which only resides in our own eyes. Remove the cloud from before your eyes and the sun becomes visible, get rid of the *mūdhadṛsti* or the perverted vision and you will realize Brahma. Spinoza's process of God realization also tells the same thing. He classifies knowledge into three categories of imagination, reason and intuition. The first is tainted and perverted; it only reads diversions in the world of body and mind. It is unable to realize God Who is the all pervasive whole, both of essence and existence. But when we prepare ourselves to know by reason and intuition, it is clear to us that all forms of thought and extension live, move and have their being in God.

Rabindranath writes in *Sādhanā*: "Untruth there certainly is, not in the system of the universe, but in our power of comprehension."[31] How, then, are we to know the truth? The exact answer will be, by elevating our power of comprehension. Through knowledge only, lies the redemption of our vision. Man's excellence consists in 'enlarging his consciousness by growing with and growing into his

---

31. *Sadhana*, p. 140.

surroundings.'[32] We grow big by knowing the essence in all things. This is what is called by Spinoza to 'now the cause of things. Neither to weep, nor to laugh at the world, it is of no avail to curse or coax our fate. Only when we understand things by their first causes, we get enlightenment and our life is emancipated. '*Bhūtéṣu bhūtéṣu bichintya*' By realizing him in each and all' as the Upanisads speak of it.

Spinoza's reason leads us to comprehend things *sub specie aeternitatis*. It annihilates time and goes beyond all petty passions and preoccupations. Under the vast expanse of the one, the many are known. All our emotions vanish, all our sufferings disappear when we come to realize our joys and sorrows, our thought and existence as a part of the vast and eternal order. This realization unites us with the whole, and complete peace follows from it. *té sarbagam sarbatah prāpyadhirāh yūktātmanah sarbamébābhiśanti* The Rishis were they who having reached the supreme God from all sides, had found abiding peace, had become united with all, had entered into the life of the Universe. The Upanisads are replete with the exaltations of this union. By union with all only can we be free from all agony and thus redeemed, can we realize God. The following two hymns of the Ishopanisad also harp at the same idea.

Yastū sarbāṇi bhūtāni ātmanyabānupasyanti,
sarbabhūtésū ātmānam tato na bijūgūpsaté 161
Yasmin sarbani atmaibabhūtbijanatah,
tatra ko moha kah soka ékatwamanūpaśyati 171

'The wise man who perceives all beings as not distinct from his own self at all, and his own self as the self of every being, he does not, by virtue of that perception, hate anyone. What delusion, what sorrow is there for the wise man who sees the unity of existence and perceives all beings as his own self.'

The Western mind suffers from the mania of possession. His delight is in conquering a thing. Thus he conquers land, conquers space and time, conquers nature. In politics he conquers other man to his own dominion; in society he conquers his neighbours to his own advantage; in religion, he conquers the pagans to the Holy Kingdom.

---

32. *Ibid*, p. 4.

His philosophy is thus individualistic singing the glory of the isolated individual who owns the world by conquest. But the man of the East has always glorified union. Instead of conquering things to submission, he has realized his greatness by uniting himself with the *Brahma* or the larger whole. Quoting Rabindranath again, "Man's superiority in the scale of creation is not in power of possession, but in the power of union."[33] And this spirit of union has been the creed of the East. Spinoza, by his union with all by conceiving them under eternity comes very near to the Eastern thought.

Knowing things *sub specie aeternitatis*, man knows himself to be in God and God to be in Himself. He becomes a God. Indian philosophy also tells us the same thing. Knowing God and his eternal laws, we also know ourselves as God. *Brahmabid brahmaiba bhabati* — The knower of Brahma becomes Brahma himself — says the Māndukya. Isopanisad makes it still clear when it says, *Tat té pasyāmi ekatwamanū pashytah*. Through thy grace, I behold the most blessed form of Thine. I am indeed He, that Being who dwells there'. This is known as the union of the individual soul with the universal soul. Rabindranath's poetic terms *jeebanadébatā* and *viswadébatā* also convey the same meaning.

Through this realization, follows bliss. Spinoza has called it beatitude. In his Siddhanta Vindusara, Shankara speaks of Brahma as bliss only *Brahmaiba Kébalam.* Also we find in the Upanisad, *sarbabyāpi sa bhagabān tasmāt sarbagatah ebah* 'The supreme being is all pervading, therefore he is the innate good of all. The wise realize God as love. *Raso bai sah*!

In the middle of the fifth part of *Ethic*, Spinoza passes on to the consideration of those matters which appertain to the duration of the mind without relation to the body. By this he conceives of a state, when mind can be fully detached from the body. This is the mental state which Gerald Heard calls 'alert passivity', and Carpenter calls 'consciousness without thought'. A similar state of mind also is pointed out in Vedanta. What it means by *utkrānti* is nothing but a temporary state of mind when it is totally separated from the body. Spinoza's intuition is not foreign to the Indian thought. The Vedanta

---

33. *Sadhana*, p. 9.

places *dibyadristi* as the highest type of knowledge and makes God-realization possible only through this.

Melamed has devoted a whole book to prove that Spinoza is more akin to Buddha than to any one of the Western thinkers. He has laboriously written a whole chapter to show, by linking up various religious movements, how the Buddhistic philosophy has been handed down to Spinoza. Against Melamed, this much will suffice to say that the same truth may have occurred to two thinkers of two different ages. Philosophical conviction is not communicated from one country to another so easily as Melamed fancies and served ready-made.

We do find many similar points in Buddha and Spinoza, not because the former was the philosophical ancestor of the latter, but because both were men of great thought and vision. Both were born in like surroundings, suffering from the sway of ceremony and superstition. Both revolted against the religious rites and sacrifices, against propitiating the gods to incur blessedness. Both held that the world is neither good nor bad, neither heartless nor irrational, neither perfect nor beautiful. But, they held, 'it is man's anthropomorphism that makes him look upon the cosmic process as a sort of human activity.'[34]

The Nirvāna of Nagarjuna has much similarity with Spinoza's Substance. The Mahayana School also believes in the immanence of Reality. Yamakami Sagen writes, "Buddhism acknowledges the presence, in this world, of a reality which transcends the bond of phenomena, which is immanent everywhere, and in which we live and move and have our being."[35]

To live *sub specie aeternitatis* can be compared with what Buddha called *Brahma Vihāra* or living, moving and having ones joy in Brahma. According to Spinoza, every man has, in his mind, the capacity to have the perfect knowledge about things; in other words, every man bears within him the possibility of God realization. In *Parinibbāna Sutta*, we hear Buddha telling his disciples: "Every living being possesses the essential germs of Buddhahood." We also find in Buddhism, a reference to Spinoza's universal love. Aryadéva,

34. Radhakrishnan, Indian Philosophy Vol. I, p. 456.
35. Systems of Buddhistic Thought, p. 64.

an authentic interpreter of later Buddhism writes, "Whosoever feels a universal love for his fellow creatures will rejoice in conferring bliss on them and by so doing, attain *Nirvāna*."

What is this *Nirvana*? Does it mean total extinction? Does it recommend death as an escape from the pangs of worldly miseries? Many recent scholars including Rhys *David deny* that *Nirvāna* means total death. To them, it signifies the divine life of no attachment, a life of love and service. In fact, Buddha, after his enlightenment, lived and preached his message in this world. The state of *Jibanmūkta*, *Arhat* or *sa-ūpādhiśeṣa nirvāna* point to say that *Nirvāna* is only a state of spiritual excellence, which comes after a perfect knowledge of the way to the removal of all sorrow. Nagarjuna writes, 'That which, under the influence of causes and conditions is *Samsāra*, is, when exempt from the influence of causes and conditions, to be taken as *Nirvana*. It means only the annihilation of the old for the erection of the new.' Spinoza's *amor intellectualis Dei* also knows everything to be the manifestation of the one free cause, God and in this sense only, can also be read with *Nirvana*.

Albert Schweitzer draws a similarity between Spinoza and Chuang Tzu of China.[36] Both these thinkers, he says, were at the same time realistic and mystical. The Tao of Chuang Tzu has much resemblance in scope with Spinoza's Substance. Tao is eternal and without beginning. "Before heaven and earth were, Tao was," writes Chuang Tzu. But while Spinoza prescribes a life of knowledge and action for the virtuous man, and condemns all kinds of indolence, Chuang Tzu has nothing to give but a life of inaction. "Resolve your mental energy into abstraction, your physical energy into inaction. Allow yourself to fall in with the natural order of phenomena, without admitting the element of self." Spinoza, on the contrary, glorified the power of man and said that we rejoice in so far as we act.

Indian philosophy has often been mistreated in the hands of foreign scholars who only half comprehended it. Many deride it as religion and not philosophy at all. Its aim is alleged to be salvation and not knowledge. The static universalism of the Upanisads, says Melamed, gives the picture of a dead God. Even sincere students like Schweitzer see nothing but world and life negation in it. In this sense

---

36. *Christianity and Religions of the World*, p. 58.

Melamed speaks of Spinoza more as an Eastern religionist than a Western philosopher. In this sense too, Spinoza appears a pessimist to him.

All this smacks of nothing but the unwillingness to fully understand a great thinker. Perhaps Melamed is not prepared to show as much sympathy as is necessary to understand Spinoza as well as Indian philosophy. He ignores the special import of terms used in the above books and, so misled, fabricates many supposed inconsistencies. For instance, he judges Spinoza's intellectual love in the standard of ordinary love and condemns it as the lowest kind of love, for it degenerates into a perverted self-love. This misunderstanding also compels Cousin to conclude that Spinoza "was an Indian *mūni*, a Persian Sufi, an enthusiastic monk and the author whom this pretended atheist most resembles, is the unknown author of the 'Imitation of Jesus Christ.'

Mūndaka Upanisad says that "the fetter of the heart is broken, all doubts are solved, all his (man's) works perish when He has been beheld who is high and low. (cause and effect)" Pātanjala Yoga holds the realization of the self as the supreme height the soul can fly to. In his *Vívekа Chūdāmani*, Shankara also speaks of the same truth. Realization can not come from outside, it can never materialize by invoking the good-will of any outside Deity. God is to be realized by enlarging the self by higher and higher degrees of knowledge. In this state of realization, which Samkara describes as the state of pure and unfettered *chaitanya*, the self finds itself not isolated from the world, but united with it. It is the ecstatic mental state, grown rich with the knowledge of self as a part of the Greater whole. Hence God realization does not draw the self away from the universe, it unites it with the universal self. This is what Spinoza's intellectual love of God means too. It is that state of greatness when one finds himself through knowledge, as one with the universe. This union and realization can never be grasped by those who break their brains by bringing in worldly similes. If the latter do not laugh away intuition as something unnatural and unphilosophical, they can easily understand how it is possible for the mind to soar up to such heights where all worldly barricades melt away and the one underlying essence is realized. This is what the ancient Rishis of India had realized when they sang,

Srñwantū viswe amrtasya putrāh
Vedāhamétad purusam mahāntam
Ādityabarnam tamasah parastāt
taméba biditwā atimṛtyūméti—

—"Listen to me, ye sons of the immortal spirit, ye who live in the heavenly abode, I have known the Supreme Person whose light shines forth from beyond the darkness. Knowing him I have attained immortality."

To those, to whom this remains still incomprehensible, let us speak in the words of Pascal, "Incomprehensible? But because you cannot understand a thing, it does not cease to exist."

5

The Man and His Philosophy

To be a philosopher is not merely to have subtle thoughts, or even to found a school, but so to love wisdom as to live according to its dictates a life of independence, simplicity, magnanimity and trust.

—Thoreau

Going to give an estimate of Nandalal Bose, the artist, Rabindranath begins the article with a pen-picture of Spinoza. He writes, "Spinoza was a seeker of truth. One may very well disengage his philosophy from the context of his personality and view it separately. But only when we see the two as related to each other, his works become radiantly meaningful. The Synagogue made him an outcast at the prime of his life, but even during his darkest days, he never failed to hold fast to truth. Till death, his means of livelihood was but meager; the king of France offered him a handsome pension, he only refused it. A friend of his, when he died, wanted to leave his property to Spinoza, but the latter declined it in favour of the friend's brother. Only when we hold together Spinoza the philosopher and Spinoza the man, we begin to see the real significance of his quest for truth and understand that his *Sādhanā* did not originate from the abstract intellect, but was the fruition of his entire nature."[1]

Spinoza, the man, was a clear reflection of the philosophy he drew out for the world. In the words of Rattner, he lived the ethics he wrote. To the society of philistines, who lived satisfied with patches of easy superstitions imposed from without, Spinoza's life was a

1. From his article in *Nireekshā*, 'Nandalal' Number.

challenge. Even in the teeth of adversities, it sang of the joy of a life of reason, of free contemplation and conviction. It was but natural that the contemporary society could not give room to so broad a mind as his.

Yet Spinoza, so cruelly spurned by men, did yet love them till his death. He was superbly pleasing to his friends, perseverantly considerate to his correspondents who could not understand him. He knew the weakness of man, knowing perfectly his own limitations too. Therefore, he did not, as it were from a high pedestal of wit and wisdom, hurl angry stones at the ignorant multitude. He never laughed away or weeped at the world disorders but philosophized, that is, tried to know them by their causes. In a way, he was the most sympathetic and lovable of all philosophers.

This is what Schwegler writes about Spinoza, "The cloudless purity and sublime tranquility of a perfectly wise man were mirrored in his life. Abstemious, satisfied with little, master of his passions, never immoderately sad or glad, gentle and benevolent, of a character admirably pure, he faithfully followed the doctrines of his philosophy, even in his daily life."[2]

Truth was his only one master. It was a God to him. He did not scruple to succumb to the dictates of truth even at the cost of giving up many of his pet beliefs. He 'fearlessly drew out the consequences of his first principles nowhere camouflaging their import despite the fact that they often issued in conflicts not only with religious dogma but even with the obvious appearances of everyday experience. Spinoza was never afraid of persecution nor even of appearing absurd'. His love for truth and truth alone can be illustrated by umpteen instances from his own life. He refused to dedicate a book of his to the French king, a chance which promised him material happiness. He did not accept the proposed professorship at Heidelburg, as he apprehended that he might not truly serve truth by taking to school room instructions. He was satisfied with his free school of disciples at The Hague, who got lessons from him and had the liberty of commenting on him and getting their doubts clarified.

Mammon could never entice Spinoza, even when his star was the faintest. Leibnitz played false with his philosophy and disfigured it to

2. *History of Philosophy*, p. 168.

incur the pleasure of the court. Kant also once submitted to the German authorities and avoided state persecution by suppressing his own free assertions. But any fear of any kind was foreign to Spinoza. Philosophy was more than his life to him, and he did never stoop on the way of free expression. Martinue writes, "His metaphysic may be strange but his love of truth was transparent, and his candour met no resistance from pride. His virtues, no doubt, were mainly of the type which Aristotle calls 'dianoetic' in which thought takes the lead and will follows."[3]

Spinoza gave life to philosophy and rescued it from the dreariness of scholasticism. The most mature book of his is called '*Ethic*', signifying the close connection that philosophy bears with life. The excellence of a philosopher does not lie in making abstract and categorical enunciations. To borrow a saying from Radhakrishnan, "To form man is the object of philosophy."[4] Human wisdom is misused if it only exhausts itself in breath-taking questions which have no connection with life. Wisdom we have enough, only how far we can live by that wisdom is the main question facing us today. As Mahatma Gandhi writes, "The world does not hunger for Shastras. What it craves and will always crave is sincere action."[5] Spinoza had never flown off life. In fact, he based his metaphysics upon his ethics and not vice versa.

Spinoza's personality was a happy harmony of knowledge and action. He knew the causes of things and thus getting the required knowledge, engraved it first on the plane of his daily life. He earned his own livelihood. Being a lover of free thought, he gave the same rights to others also. He never imposed himself upon those round him, either materially or intellectually. Everett writes, "Spinoza was preeminently the type of the scholar, one to whom the search for an understanding of the world and of human life was infinitely precious. No one has surpassed him in devotion to this ideal. And with this is joined a quality, not always found in speculative thinkers, which marks him as a moral leader. This is the unwavering conviction that truth, at whatever cost, has immediate and direct application to the

---

3. Study of Spinoza, p. 105.
4. *My Search for Truth*, p 34.
5. Harijan, 3.3.1946.

conduct of life. It is not a treasure to be kept in the cloister guarded as a possession of the elite. This conviction he shares with other moral leaders of the human race—with Buddha, Socrates and Jesus."

Spinoza's intellectual pursuit was never utilitarian in character. His philosophy was not for any one, not even for his own glory and fame. Knowing as far as he could, he did not hide his ignorance of things he did not know. And so he never boasted having found the best philosophy. In a letter, he wrote, "I do not presume that I have found the best philosophy. I know that I have found the true philosophy." To the portals of wisdom and knowledge he came with the simplicity of a child and feasted upon as much gift as was given to him by truth. In one of his letters to Blyenburg, Spinoza makes explicit his dispassionate longing for knowledge: "[...] Even if I have once to find untrue the fruits of my natural understanding, they would make me happy, since I enjoy them, and I endeavour to pass my life not in sorrow and sighs, but in peace, joy and cheerfulness and thereby I ascend one step higher."

And the truest vision, ever had of God, as Renan put it, had come to Spinoza. Merz writes: "In Spinoza, philosophy attained an elevation of spirit and diction which has only been reached in rare instances. It became to its author an expression, as it were, of his deepest religious convictions; it rose to inspiration. Such had been the philosophy of Plato in antiquity, such was the philosophy of Spinoza in modern times. Both are conspicuous in their grandeur and sublimity."[6]

Let us conclude the chapter with an appreciation by Schleiermacher, "The sublime spirit of the world penetrated him, the infinite was his beginning and his end; the universal his only and eternal love; living in holy innocence and profound humility, he contemplated himself in eternal world, and saw that he, too, was for that world a mirror worthy of love; he was full of religion and full of the holy spirit."[7]

---

6. History of European Thought in the 19th century, Vol. III p. 331.
7. Redė über die Religion, p. 47.

6

The Eternal Spinoza

Many are the paths that rise
To the hill-top, but when we
Reach the hill-top, then our eyes
Universal moonlight see.

—A Japanese Buddhist Poem

"In my father's house there are many mansions', only to reach any one of them, are needed the wings of a genuine sacred transport. These wings Spinoza had...., his foot is on the vera vita, his eye on the beatific vision."

Now that we have come to this last part of our journey, we have to give our final label to Spinoza before pitching our last milestone.

We have been acquainted with Spinoza's philosophy from all its facets; its world picture, its psychological explanations and its verdicts on the properties and possibilities of the human mind. Now, naturally, comes the time to give a name to the thoughts of the great thinker.

We are very fond of labels and names. It has often been a pleasure for the critics to bring down a philosopher under one of the many convenient types and know him by that type only. Then, what is the name we would wish to give Spinoza? Can it be pantheism, monotheism or atheism? Does his philosophy propose many gods, one God or no God at all? Restless critics like Melamed have worried over not to find a definite name for Spinoza. For Melamed, Spinoza baffles all his catchwords. He writes, "Purely philosophical thought is either an affirmation or negation. Spinozism teaches both oneness and multitudinousness, rationalism and mysticism. Spinoza is a paradoxical phenomenon."[1] In another place, he remarks that Spinoza's is the 'most fascinating idea-poem recited to man'. Is it, then, such that it contains something of everything, and yet nothing particularly of anything?

One is apt to be bewildered at the versatility of Spinoza's flow of thought. It is, therefore, impossible, rather puerile, to squeeze him to any of our preconceived moulds. In fact, what are the real characteristics of the various types and isms we have fabricated out for our convenience of 'doing a philosopher? (as an American traveller is said to do a country within the shortest possible time). The isms are ever changing and shaped differently by every hand that handles them. Pantheism varies in colour with each of the professed pantheists. Same is also the case with monotheism and atheism. The latter name has often been given to one who professes a religion other than one's own. Then, it is no wonder that Spinoza was called an atheist and also a God-intoxicated saint by persons of the same age. And this often happens with every great thinker who rises above the assumed types and aspires to dwell in the entire stretch of life. They are unique in themselves. Their own type includes only a single thinker, only themselves. This is why Gunn draws out the following magnificient conclusion regarding Spinoza, "Better it is to leave labels, whether they be Theist, pantheist or Atheist. Call him just Spinoza; abandon the fruitless attempt to fit his unique views into prearranged moulds of thought and endeavour, instead, to understand him and appreciate his message as a whole."[2]

Spinoza, to repeat a sentence from a previous chapter was an 'odd' philosopher of the 17th century. On coming to the verge of our journey's end, we would like to ask: What has Spinoza to give us in our times? If we can get something in Spinoza which still sheds much light on the present age, then only can he live again. A philosopher becomes immortal by his immortal thoughts, his eternal wealth of ideas that brings inspiration to all men of all times.

This is how White, in the preface to his translation of the *Ethic*, draws up an estimate of our time. He writes, " The decay of religion,

---

1. Spinoza and Buddha, p. 26.
2. Benedict Spinoza, p. 121.

amongst other innumerable evils, has also brought upon this evil that the purely intellectual with no reference whatever to the ethical is the sole subject of research and a man devotes all his life to the anatomy of lepidoptera and never gives an hour to the solution of the problem how he may best bring insurgent and tyrannous desires under subjection or face misfortune. [...] Ethical science, strictly so called, is not existent. No preacher preaches it, the orthodox churches are given over to a philosophy of rags and 'free pulpits do nothing but mince and mash up for popular ears common places upon books and passing events. Neither does any school teach it. It is frightful to think that at the present moment, the only ethic known to the great mass of the children of this earth is a dim and decaying dread left over by a departed religion. The germinating spot in all the dangers ahead of us is the divorce of the intellect from its chief use, so that it stands itself upon curiosities, trifles, the fine arts and science, and never in ethical service." We are suffering from the tyranny of our own intellect. We suffer because we do not know, or only half-know the things we have created. The gigantic creations elude the control of man who is helpless to call a halt to their rapacious operations. After the dark fog of anthropomorphism, we are now groping in the cold night of mechanomorphism (as Gerald Heard has put it.) We have art, science and philosophy; we have, at our disposal, all the resources to make our lives pleasant and plentiful. But without a mind, without clear ethical judgement, we have but an atrophy of all our wealth, wisdom and worship.

Our inventions of power have recoiled upon us in the form of dreadful wars and killings. Our unending additons to the amenities of life bring us everything but happiness. Our mind has been a victim to abnormality, there is disease and decay all around, there is mutual ill-feeling and hatred in all our walks in society. And what is the way out of all this dirt and dross? How can we learn the art of being men?

By being more human. By tolerance, by understanding, by accepting the whole world of existence. By coming together, meeting together and working together. More and still more understanding is the imperative way out, it is the yearning need of our time. And all these words we have come across in the vocabulary of Spinoza. He cries for less condemnation, less despair, and appeals for an iota of more understanding. Understanding is love and by love can we be retrieved. "Minds are not conquered by arms," he emphasizes, "but by love and generosity." His non-violence is still a crying need of our times. He superseded Kropotkin in his acclaimation of blessed anarchism which visualized a happy community of men living by mutual aid and no outside legislation. 'Man is a God to man' and there will cease to be any conflict in society if all men could be led to live by reason and reason alone. Spinoza had little hope in the vehement plans of changing man by changing the material environment. This change is not as easy as it is said. It requires a long and difficult process of self-education, and knowing oneself vis-à-vis the world is always the highest education. Not man, alone and insulated, but man in the universe is, with Spinoza, the kernel of all realization.

Reason leads us to religion. Union with men by social piety raises us to feel the spirit of God. Men are not to be considered as so many worms or insects. We can only unite with them as one among them. To know this, to know oneself *sub specie aeternitatis* leads us to the intellectual love of God. This love is Spinoza's religion, and its reward is beatitude. It is that state of faith which comes after complete understanding. This religion is also a modern necessity. This is the religion of life as Julian Huxley has put it. Rabindranath calls it the 'religion of man'. Schweitzer would call it 'reverence for life'. Quoting from Radhakrishnan, "Religion is not a simple spiritual state of the individual. It is the practice of the divine rule among men." Again, more vivid, a deeper sense of the one universal God is the profoundest need of our age.[3]

Spinoza's religion also sang the divine excellence of life upon earth. It is this religion that can only lead us through our sorry travails. We agree with H. G Wells, when he writes, "The new religion of the coming man demands the subordination of the self, of the aggressive personality to the common creative task, which is the conquest and animation of the universe by life. It denies the existence of an anthropomorphic God and it can not afford to recognize any prevaricating use of the word God. That word implies a personality or it implies nothing."[4]

---

3. The Religion We Need, p. 32.
4. The Conquest of Time.

Spinoza lives again. He is as modern as any of the living thinkers. In fact, the great truths of the great leaders of thought are never old, they hold a ready receptacle in all times. So also has Spinoza never been old, immortal till his thoughts are. As E. S. Smith concludes, "At the close of the three centuries which have passed since Spinoza lived in exile, a great teacher with no pupils, unnumbered thousands reverence his teachings today. Though we sense the modernism of Spinoza, perhaps the truer name for it is 'timelessness'. When an age sees itself reflected in the words of an old thinker, it calls him modern forgetting that the universal is ageless."[5]

The desperate search for an irreproachably perfect type is the way of the pessimist. Being imperfect himself, he hopefully goes out to find out the most perfect. The result is that he is disappointed and takes consolation in an unrealizable Utopia. He can see only defects in all the philosophies he comes across. He rejects each one of them and is self-satisfied by using invectives at them. This has been Melamed's fate. He is out with set moulds and types that lie in his own imagination and finding Spinoza something exceptional and ill-fitting to his idea patterns, he denounces him as an Eastern visionary, full of paradoxical phenomena.

Descartes had started with doubt and disbelief and hence he could only be sure of himself. And improving upon this *cogito-ergo-sum* hypothesis, he had but to bring in superimposing dogmas. One cannot doubt and live at the same time. Rejecting all, one can never find anything left for him. Rejection is always negative. It is also a misnomer as we are already born a part of this universe. Rejection reduces man to the chrysalis cave of the Diogenian type of individualism; politically to his own interested group, and in morals, to his pet dogmas. The excellence, in the eyes of the modern age, lies in assimilation and acceptance, accepting the whole of existence as it is. And Spinoza lives eternally as a minister of this spirit of reconciliation.

Spinoza's Reality has three synonymous names. "The conception of Nature is scientific, expressive of a certain unity among phenomena, that of God is religious, marking a living unity of cause;

---

5. Spinoza Quarterly, Tercentenary Issue, p. 101.

that of Substance is metaphysical, indicating a unity of ground."[6] His science recognizes the realm of faith and his religion, again, does not overlook our world of sense perception. In the same breath Spinoza denies asceticism and pleasure-mad worm-life. He equally avoids 'exuberant violence of will, sentimental emotionalism and cold loveless struggle for wisdom. While recommending a life of joy through one's own power of reason and love, Spinoza does not forget to give bread and all decent amenities their due place in life. We can never run away from worldly attachments. Swami Vivekananda has said, "Both attachment and detachment perfectly developed makes a man great and happy."[7] A life of detached attachments, if the antinomy can be allowed, is also what Spinoza has prescribed for the man in society.

This synthesis in Spinoza, this viewing of life as a whole, also appealed to many great thinkers who came after Spinoza. Hoeffding writes, "In him all lines of thought converge, mysticism and naturalism, theoretical and practical interests. His book is not merely a speculative work, but a work of art." Professor Demos says that in Spinoza we find a combination of abstract with the concrete. Spinoza is at once a stimulus to one's intellect and guide to one's life; his system is reason transformed to wisdom. And as Heine, the German scholar of repute and also an admirer of Spinoza had put it, "All our modern philosophers, though often perhaps unconsciously, see through the glasses which Baruch Spinoza ground."

Spinoza's way of realization takes into account all ways and means and gives them due importance. For the philosopher, he has his rigid *sādhāna* of reason. But for the average man, he leaves the rather easier process of faith and self-submission. And side by side, the life he lives glorifies the realization through action. Spinoza's has been the harmony of knowledge, faith and action.

Romain Rolland has called Spinoza *The European Krishna*. Spinoza's harmony in philosophy can be called in Indian terms, the one of Jnāna, Bhakti and Karma. The Indian Krishna of yore was also a great leader of harmony and reconciliation. With him, all the gold in various schools of ancient Indian philosophy were wreathed, as it

6. Martinue's, p. 17.
7. Letters of Swami Vivekananda, p. 405.

were, into a beautiful garland. His Bhagabadgeetā is a great hymn of synthesis. It recognizes the worth of all the Yogas and assures God-realization to one who is firmly established in either. In the fifth hymn of the fifth chapter, Krishna says to Arjuna,

Yat sāmkhyaih prāpyaté sthānam tat yogairapi gamyaté
Ékam sāmkyam cha yogam cha yah paśyati sa paśyati

'The supreme state, which is reached by the Sāmkhya Yogi, is attained also by the Karmayogi. Therefore, he who sees Samkhyayoga and Karmayoga as one, as far as their result goes, really sees."